The Australian Heritage Cookbook

A collection of recipes and memories from Australian kitchens

bay books

The Australian Heritage Cookbook

Published by Bay Books® an imprint of Murdoch Books Pty Limited.

Murdoch Books Australia
Pier 8/9, 23 Hickson Road, Millers Point NSW 2000
Phone: +61 (0)2 8220 2000 Fax: +61 (0)2 8220 2558

Author: Joy Hayes
Design: Anne Marie Cummins and Justin Thomas for Uber Creative
Photography: Phil Wymant
Food Stylist: Ann Creber
Home Economist: Judy Simmons
Editorial Co-ordinator: Anna Goodwin
Production: Monika Vidovic
Project Co-ordinator: Sarah Aitken
Originally published as *Australian Family Circle Heritage Cookbook*
ISBN 1-74045-556 8

Printed by Sun Fung Offset Binding Company Limited in 2004. PRINTED IN CHINA

IMPORTANT: Those who might be at risk from the effects of salmonella poisoning should consult their doctor with any concerns about eating raw eggs.

Special thanks to Viscopy and the following Art Galleries for their assistance in the use of paintings reproduced in this publication – Art Gallery of New South Wales, National Gallery of Victoria, Melbourne, National Gallery of Australia, Bathurst Regional Art Gallery.

Right:
John Skinner Prout
1806-1876
(Bush landscape with waterfall and an aborigine stalking native animals, New South Wales, 1860's)
Oil on canvas 70.5 x 91.4cm
Purchased under the terms of the Florence Turner Blake bequest 1976
Art Gallery of New South Wales

Previous page:
Margaret Preston
1875-1963
Summer
Oil on canvas 51 x 51cm
purchased 1920
Art Gallery of New South Wales

Following page:
Eugene von Guérard
Sydney heads, 1865
Oil on canvas 56 x 94cm
Bequest of Major H.W. Hall 1974
Art Gallery of New South Wales

W. B. Gould 1801-1853
Flower Piece
Oil on canvas 65.8 x 76.8cm
purchased 1956
Art Gallery of New South Wales

Contents

Tom Roberts 1856–1931
The Golden Fleece: Shearing at Newstead 1894
Oil on canvas 104 x 158.7cm
purchased 1894
Art Gallery of New South Wales

Introduction

In a world of fast food, instant meals and eating on the run it is difficult to imagine an era when meal times were relaxed, social occasions.

The pleasures of a leisurely picnic and the enjoyment of a large Sunday roast now seem nothing more than a memory to today's time-starved families.

Tastes have also changed as pre-packed, foil-wrapped sachets replace the market fresh produce that was the hallmark of previous generations of cooks.

Yet, with only a little time and effort, it is possible to once again experience the robust flavours and warm atmosphere that were so characteristic of this bygone culinary era.

The Australian Heritage Cookbook gives a brief account of the history of Australian food and eating habits as they have developed since 1788. It charts the development of recipes from basic settler foods to the more lavish tastes of later years which absorbed tastes and influences from all over the world.

Many recipes have stood the test of time, and several dishes which the early settlers relied upon to keep them going through the hard times, or simply remind them of their home country, can be recreated in a modern kitchen with no loss of flavour. All recipes have been updated to allow for modern cooking methods and ingredients, and have been tested in our kitchens.

Accompanying the recipes and providing added insight into the customs and tastes of the time is a wide selection of Australian paintings, all chosen for their relevance to Australia's culinary history.

The Australian Heritage Cookbook is truly a veritable feast for the senses and will transport you to a world of charm, beauty and good taste.

The First Hundred Years

Margaret Preston 1875–1963
Adam & Eve in the Garden of Eden 1950
Gouache stencil on black card
50.1 x 49.5cm
purchased 1950
Art Gallery of New South Wales

The First Hundred Years

Food was in the forefront of Captain Arthur Phillip's mind in 1788 when he ordered one of the first buildings, a bakehouse, to be constructed on the proposed site of Sydney town. The First Fleet of sailing ships had anchored in Botany Bay at 4 am on 20th January, but Phillip selected Sydney Cove as a more suitable spot for settlement because of its shelter and a stream christened the Tank Stream.

Without adequate food and water there was little chance of survival for the remnants of the 1500 people who had set out from Plymouth to establish a penal settlement in Australia. The stark journey of 12,000 miles had taken eight long, hazardous months.

The flotilla consisted of the warships Sirius and Supply, six transports and three store ships. It carried a mixed company of British seamen, soldiers, officials and a wretched collection of 568 male and 191 female convicts, plus nine children, outcasts from the poorest parts of Great Britain. The appetites of these people and their descendants formed the nucleus of the Australian way of eating which developed over the next 200 years. Their longing for the familiar 18th century dishes of their homeland, such as roast beef and Yorkshire pudding, Irish stew, Scotch eggs, Welsh rarebit, steamed suet pudding and treacle tart, were to be realised when the supply ships at last began to service the promised land, agriculture and grazing had developed, and the hungry years were over. The fact that the diet they craved was totally unsuitable for the climate and conditions in which the settlers found themselves was unimportant to them. The nostalgic image transcended common sense, and it seems that knowledge of nutrition, or any inventive cookery skills were sadly lacking among them.

Captain Phillip's cargo had included cattle, sheep, goats, pigs, poultry, seeds and cuttings, and farm tools, as well as food supplies. But the livestock intended for breeding either escaped, died or was slaughtered to feed the starving. The first pitiful crops sown in desperation in this unfriendly soil not surprisingly faded away, and in any case there were only two farmers in the group.

One soldier and 36 convicts had died on the journey. Those who disembarked were debilitated from malnutrition, vitamin-deficiency diseases, fever, dysentery, confinement and hardship. The unskilled convicts, mainly hardened criminals brutalised by their treatment, were totally unfitted for work and disinclined to contribute to their own survival.

The food supplies had been planned to last for two years. They consisted of flour, rice, salt beef and pork, dried peas, oatmeal, butter, cheese and vinegar. For two years there was hardly any fresh meat or familiar fresh fruit or vegetables and for four years, no fresh milk. Flour and grains were weevilly, transported butter and cheese melted and became rancid in the heat. Fish were plentiful but there were no boats and no real desire to build any. Kangaroos and other wild game and birds were hard to catch; unfamiliar fruits and plants were suspect. Governor Phillip's weekly rations for an adult male were: 7lb bread or flour, 7lb salt beef or 4lb salt pork, 2 lb dried peas, 6 oz butter, ½ lb rice.

Phillip built a hospital and a garden on the slopes adjacent to the bakehouse which serviced the marine encampment and the convicts' tent settlement. One

'We are near Australia! Can't you smell the flowers?' But the realities of living there turned into a nightmare for the newcomers.

woman wrote home: *We are comforted with the hopes of a supply of tea from China, and flattered with getting riches when the settlement is complete, and the hemp which the place produces is brought to perfection. Our kingaroo rats are like mutton, but much leaner; and there is a kind of chickweed so much in taste like our spinach that no difference can be discerned. Something like ground ivy is used for tea, but a scarcity of salt and sugar makes our best meals insipid.* [1]

There was rum, of course, to dull their senses and make them forget their misery. It was a fiery spirit distilled from grain in Bengal and often used as barter instead of money. Governor Phillip had tried to control the rum trade, but after his departure in 1792, illicit trading flourished under successive officials and profiteers who became rich on the proceeds as fast as their consumers, convicts and trusties, revelled in drunkenness and depravity.

Meanwhile Governor Phillip and his lieutenants had celebrated Christmas 1788, their first in Australia, with a meal of roast goose, mince pies and Stilton cheese.

The bewildered aborigines who witnessed the strange behaviour and eating habits of these intruders must have wondered why so many of them were starving. The original aboriginal cuisine was perfectly balanced nutritionally for the nomadic family tribes who fished, hunted and gathered their food with nets, harpoons and spears wherever they wandered. But eating flying foxes, snakes, lizards, goannas, bandicoots, possum eggs, rats, caterpillars, witchetty grubs, moths, and crocodiles, dugong, wild roots, grasses, berries and pods didn't appeal to the British. They grudgingly cooked kangaroo, possum, wallaby, wild duck, pigeon and turkey from necessity. But they made no attempt to understand why the aborigines had appeared happy and well-nourished when their Garden of Eden was invaded, and proceeded to kill them off, decimate them with introduced diseases, brutalise them or use them as slaves.

In those days Australia was a land of great forests, soft-footed animals, rich plant life and perfumed flowers. The Australian writer Mary Gilmore, recalled her grandmother telling her that seamen used to say its scent was akin to the Spice Islands', and voyagers would call to one another as their ships approached her shores, 'We are near Australia! Can't you smell the flowers?' But the realities of living there turned into a nightmare for the newcomers.

By 1790, when the notorious Second Fleet landed, weekly rations for the colony's adults had been reduced to 2 ½lb flour, 2 1b pork and 2 1b rice. By that time the colony was close to starvation, the soldiers and convicts alike emaciated and exhausted. Faced with disaster, Governor Phillip had despatched Sirius to Cape Town in October, 1788 for emergency supplies, but after seven months away, her crew returned with only enough to last a further four months.

The situation was desperate, as one man recalled: *The pork and rice were brought with us from England; the pork had been salted between three and four years and every grain of rice was a moving body from the inhabitants lodged within it. We soon left off boiling the pork which had become so old and dry that it shrunk one half in its dimensions when so dressed. Our usual method of cooking was to cut off the daily morsel and toast it on a fork before the fire, catching the drops which fell on a slice of bread or in a saucer of rice. Our flour was the remnant of what was brought from the Cape and was good. Instead of baking it, soldiers and convicts used to boil it up with greens.*

Dismal as the prospect was, things began to improve. In 1810, Dr Joseph Arnold noted that: *a person coming to Sydney Cove would think himself in the midst of a large city; if he dines on shore he finds all the luxury and elegance of the finest English tables.*[2]

Meanwhile, as the colony staggered from its knees, a style of bush cookery began to emerge, forming the basis

[1] *Watkin Tench, An account of the Settlement of Port Jackson in New South Wales. London, 1793.*
[2] *Louisa Anne Meredith. Notes and Sketches of NSW during a residence in the Colony. London, 1844.*

Margaret Preston 1875–1963
Black cockatoos c. 1925
Hand coloured woodcut
24.8 x 25.3cm
Australian National Gallery,
Canberra

Margaret Preston 1875–1963
Still Life
Woodcut, hand-coloured
12.7 x 12.5cm
purchased 1976
Art Gallery of New South Wales

of a national diet. Flour, meat, sugar, tea and salt were the commodities. Fried or grilled beef or mutton, damper sometimes spread with golden syrup or 'bullocky's joy', and billy tea with plenty of sugar were the foods, supplemented with plenty of alcohol.

The importation of sheep and cattle, the success of land grants, grazing and agriculture, and the fruits and vegetables produced on the fertile river flats at Parramatta promised happier times. Elizabeth and John Macarthur built Elizabeth Farm at Parramatta in 1792 and conducted a highly successful farming estate there. When Governor Phillip returned home, 7000 acres were allotted to 1200 amateur farmers; 140 were convicts.

Adventurers, squatters, settlers, itinerant bushmen, shearers, timbergetters, whalers and sealers made up a drifting population outside the settlements and towns. Danish dairy experts, Swedes, Yugoslavs, Hungarians, French and German immigrants arrived and began to make their contributions to dairying, food and wine production. But in 1798, most. of the population were still dependent on government rations. In 1803, the first settlers in Hobart were faced with hunger too, but they must have been more industrious and disposed to helping themselves in the more familiar climate. They developed their horticultural, dairying, brewing and meat industries. They farmed, introduced bees, grew pretty gardens, developed orchards and introduced a flourishing weekly market for settlers' produce as well as exporting wheat and many other food commodities to New South Wales. These people also showed more imagination in their cookery and seemed to make the best they could of wild meats. A Tasmanian dish called Grabber Gullen Pie was a hollowed out pumpkin filled with possum meat and baked in the coals. They fried kangaroo tail and called it Pan Jam, made kangaroo pasties, and a dish called Slippery Bob—kangaroo brains in batter, fried in emu fat.

In 1812, when young Maria Macarthur, a daughter of Governor Gidley King, and new wife of Hannibal Macarthur, John Macarthur's nephew, was setting up her household on a grand scale at Parramatta, Sydney was still a village with oak trees and grass on the footpaths and men in cabbage tree hats in the streets. At The Vineyard, the Macarthur estate, there were picnics, boating on the river, walking, jam making parties and in the evening, singing and dancing. One of the six Macarthur daughters recalled: *Necessaries of all kinds were by that time procurable in Sydney. The orders for The Vineyard were for large quantities. We had huge jars some three feet high for rice and raw sugar, etc. Loaves of sugar ranged on shelves, raisins and currants wholesale. Tea came direct in chests from William Leslie in Canton with many other good things, ginger, coffee and chocolate. Bread was baked at home. Dairy produce came from Sydney. A butcher at the farm killed our own sheep, 'good beef could be procured at Parramatta. Fruit and vegetables ad libitum. In the fruit season a large tray was placed on the sideboard in the dining room prepared for any fruit lover through the day.*

The cellar was filled with casks of English beer, and sherry, marsala and port on draught. Lamps were lit with whale oil, wax candles came from England and tallow ones were made on the farm. The maids were Scottish, the menservants English or Indian immigrants. Convicts were used for outdoor work but never allowed to cross the threshold of the house.

Meals were based on Mrs Beeton's cookbook, which was published in England in 1861 by S. O. Beeton. Maria received from her godmother in England, a long letter of advice on household management with menus, recipes and table plans.[3] These were based on the *Service á la Francaise* fashionable at the time, in which all dishes were set out on the table, with some removed and replaced. This custom changed to the more popular *Service á la Russe*, in which dishes were served in successive courses as they are today. Maria's godmother suggested menus for Social Dinners, A Tolerable Sized Party, A Grand Dance, A Sociable Sandwich, Dinner after an Excursion, and other types of meals, as well as a menu for the simple repast shown overleaf.

By 1840, two years before Sydney became a city, it was reported by one visitor that: *There are several good inns in Sydney . . . at about double the expense in a first rate*

A Family Dinner with 2 or 3 Friends – or more.

Boiled Fish
Oyster Sauce
Vegetables • Salad • Vegetables
Plain Butter
Roast Beef

Remove the Fish and put on a Dish of Scotch Collops – remove the Salad for a Tart.

English hotel; and whilst you are served with King's Pattern plate and by about half a dozen waiters, you miss many of the common comforts.[4]

In 1843, Thomas Hamblett informed his mother in England by letter: *Today we had for dinner the leg o f a kangaroo, being the first one we have shot. It is very good eating once in a way, but I should not like to live long on it. The parrots make very good pies equal to pigeon but it seems very extravagant to eat such well dressed Ladies and Gents.*

Another dinner party menu reported in a Sydney newspaper society column in 1846, consisted of: *Wallaby tail soup followed by boiled schnapper with oyster sauce, haunch of kangaroo, wonga wonga pigeon with bread sauce, and a dessert of plantains, loquats, guavas, mandarins, pomegranates and cherimoyas.*

With the Gold Rush in 1851, the economy began to explode. Adventurers, confidence men, and speculators from all over the world joined the gold hungry population who threw up everything to go to the Victorian goldfields. Among them were thousands of Chinese, either from China or runaways who had been employed as indentured labourers in New South Wales. Industrious and tenacious, many of them began successful market gardens, greengrocers' shops or restaurants, or found work as cooks when gold fever subsided. They introduced us to steamed rice and stir-fried vegetables and are partly responsible for the great Australian fondness for Chinese food which has become part of our culinary heritage.

By 1852, theatres, hotels, restaurants, cafes, clubs, inns and taverns had multiplied, and the road between Sydney and Melbourne, a journey of six days by coach or fifteen on horseback, *was studded with taverns of one class or another*, according to one traveller.

At the end of the first 100 years of colonisation, there was general prosperity as the country moved towards Federation and its first Parliament. But it was still a male community which hadn't changed much for women since 1836, when an Adelaide woman, Mary Thomas, wrote home to her brother in England: You *will realise that housekeeping is no joke here*, probably one of the understatements of the century.

[3] *Advice to a Young Lady in the Colonies being a letter sent from Mrs. E of England to Maria Macarthur in the Colony of New South Wales in 1812. Greenhouse Publications, Pty. Ltd., 1979.*
[4] *Louisa Anne Meredith, Notes and sketches of NSW during a residence in the Colony. London, 1844.*

Joseph Lycett 1774 – 1828
The homestead at Raby c.1824
Watercolour on thick wove paper
21 x 28.5cm
National Gallery of Australia, Canberra

This small homestead, built on a free land grant of 30 acres given to convict James Ruse in 1789, was one of the first properties established around Sydney and Parramatta.

It was here that vegetables and fruit were cultivated for the colony, and strawberries were grown from offshoots of a single root that Governor Phillip had brought with him. In 1794 the first plough was introduced, and agriculture began.

Then citrus fruits and many varieties of apples and pears from Tasmania and Victoria became available, enabling industrious housewives to make jams and preserves. Our delicious Apple-Marmalade pie, picture page 89, recipe page 88, could well have been a typical dish of the time.

utmeg, Sour cream, Parsley, chopped, Croûtons, method; Peel, remove s
nd salt. Pour in just enough water to cover and cook gently, with the lic
food processor with the milks (or push through a sieve and then stir ir
over and simmer for 5-7 minutes. Serve with a swirl of sour cream anc
eparately. 750g (1/2 lb) pumpkin, 1 medium onion, chopped, 1 teaspoon
ream, Parsley, chopped, Croûtons, method; Peel, remove seeds from pum
just enough water to cover and cook gently, with the lid on, until the pu
ith the milks (or push through a sieve and then stir in the milk). Return
or 5-7 minutes. Serve with a swirl of sour cream and a sprinkling of pa
emove seeds from pumpkin, and cut into pieces. Put into a saucepan wi

Soups

s from pumpkin, and cut into pieces. Put into a saucepan with the onic
, until the pumpkin is tender. Purée the contents of the pan in a blend
e milk). Return the purée to the saucepan, adding the sugar and nutme
sprinkling of parsley on each bowl and serve a bowl of crisp croûtor
lt, Water, 2 cups milk, 2 teaspoons sugar, Pinch of grated nutmeg, So
n, and cut into pieces. Put into a saucepan with the onion and salt. Po
kin is tender. Purée the contents of the pan in a blender or food process
purée to the saucepan, adding the sugar and nutmeg. Cover and simm
ey on each bowl Sour cream, Parsley, chopped, Croûtons, method; Pe
the onion and salt. Pour in just enough water

FRENCH ONION SOUP

Serves 4

INGREDIENTS

500g (1lb) onions
60g (2oz) butter
2 vegetable or chicken stock cubes
5 cups water
1 leek, sliced
Pinch dried thyme
2 cloves garlic, crushed
Salt and freshly ground black pepper
¼ cup dry white wine
Sliced French bread
250g (8oz) Gruyère or Emmenthaler cheese, grated

METHOD

Peel onions and slice thinly. Cook very slowly, over a low heat, in the butter until soft and golden. Stir in stock cubes, water, leek, thyme, garlic, salt and pepper to taste.

Simmer, covered, for 25-30 minutes. Stir in wine. Pour into 1 large ovenproof bowl or into individual heatproof bowls. Cover with bread slices and grated cheese.

Bake in a very hot oven until cheese bubbles and becomes golden brown.

CREAM OF PUMPKIN SOUP

Serves 4

INGREDIENTS

750g (1½ lb) pumpkin
1 medium onion, chopped
1 teaspoon salt
Water
2 cups milk
2 teaspoons sugar
Pinch of grated nutmeg
Sour cream
Parsley, chopped
Croûtons

METHOD

Peel, remove seeds from pumpkin, and cut into pieces. Put into a saucepan with the onion and salt. Pour in just enough water to cover and cook gently, with the lid on, until the pumpkin is tender. Purée the contents of the pan in a blender or food processor with the milks (or push through a sieve and then stir in the milk). Return the purée to the saucepan, adding the sugar and nutmeg. Cover and simmer for 5-7 minutes.

Serve with a swirl of sour cream and a sprinkling of parsley on each bowl and serve a bowl of crisp croûtons separately.

Opposite page: French Onion Soup

KIDNEY SOUP

Serves 4-6

INGREDIENTS

6 lamb kidneys or 250g (8oz) ox kidney
60g (2oz) butter
1 small onion, finely chopped
1 small carrot, finely chopped
5 cups beef stock
1 tablespoon cornflour mixed to a paste with cold water
Salt and freshly ground pepper
4 tablespoons dry sherry
Croûtons (small squares of fried bread) to garnish

METHOD

Remove skin and fatty core from kidneys, and cut kidneys into thin slices.

Heat the butter in a heavy saucepan, add kidneys and onion, and stir until kidneys are a rich brown. Add carrot and stock, cover, and simmer for 1 hour or until kidneys are very tender.

Strain stock into a clean saucepan, discarding vegetables. Cut kidney slices into small dice and keep ready.

Heat the stock to boiling point, and stir a little into the cornflour mixture. Return this to the saucepan and stir over medium heat until smooth and boiling. Taste for seasoning, add chopped kidneys and sherry, and simmer for 1-2 minutes.

Serve in heated bowls, sprinkled with croûtons.

CHILLED TOMATO SOUP

Serves 4

INGREDIENTS

1 onion, chopped
1kg (2lb) ripe tomatoes, peeled
1 clove garlic, crushed
2 tablespoons vegetable oil
3 cups vegetable stock
1 teaspoon sugar
Salt and freshly ground pepper
1 teaspoon paprika
4 tablespoons boiled rice
Chopped parsley

METHOD

Cook the onion, tomatoes and garlic in the oil for 5 minutes. Pour on the vegetable stock, cover and simmer 10-15 minutes. Place in a blender or food processor and whizz until smooth.

Return to pan and add sugar, salt, pepper and paprika. Bring to boil and simmer 2-3 minutes. Cool and chill. Serve topped with boiled rice and chopped parsley.

MULLIGATAWNY

Serves 6

INGREDIENTS

1kg (2lb) chicken pieces, such as thighs, drumsticks, breasts
2 tablespoons plain flour
2 teaspoons curry powder
1 teaspoon turmeric
½ teaspoon ground ginger
60g (2oz) butter
6 cloves
12 peppercorns
1 large apple, peeled and diced
6 cups chicken stock
2 tablespoons lemon juice
½ cup fresh cream
Salt to taste
Boiled rice and chutney to serve

METHOD

Wipe chicken pieces with paper towels. Combine flour, curry powder, turmeric and ginger and rub well into chicken. Heat the butter in a heavy saucepan, and lightly brown the chicken on all sides. Add cloves, peppercorns, apple and stock, bring to the boil, and simmer covered for 1 hour. Remove chicken pieces, and discard peppercorns and cloves.

Skin chicken, and cut flesh into small dice. Return to soup with lemon juice and cream, gently reheat, and add salt to taste. Serve in heated bowls, with hot boiled rice and chutney offered separately to stir into the soup.

NOTE: If you wish, the soup can be whirled in a blender or food processor for a smoother texture. You might also like to add other curry accompaniments such as coconut, sultanas, or chopped peanuts, as well as the rice and chutney.

VICHYSSOISE

Serves 4

INGREDIENTS

1 leek
2 tablespoons butter
2 onions, chopped
500g (1lb) potatoes, sliced
4 cups vegetable stock
Whipped cream
Snipped chives

METHOD

Wash and slice leek and cook in the butter together with chopped onions until soft, but not brown.

Stir in sliced potatoes and stock and cook, covered, until vegetables are tender. Strain and push vegetables through a sieve. Mix well and chill thoroughly. Top with a spoonful of whipped cream sprinkled with chives just before serving.

HEARTY PEA SOUP WITH MEAT

Serves 8

INGREDIENTS

1 cup dried green peas
½ cup yellow split peas
6 cups water
3 onions, chopped
500g (1lb) potatoes, diced
1 cup sliced carrots
1 cup diced celery
1kg (2lb) pot roast or half leg of lamb
1 tablespoon whole peppercorns
2 bay leaves
2 teaspoons salt
250g (8oz) shredded cabbage
Chopped parsley

METHOD

Cover peas with cold water and allow to stand overnight. Next day, drain and place in a large saucepan with the 6 cups water.

Add onions, potatoes, carrots, celery, meat, peppercorns, bay leaves and salt. Cover and cook gently 1½ hours. Add shredded cabbage and cook 10 more minutes.

Skim fat from top.

Remove meat from soup and cut into slices. Serve either on a plate with the soup or cut pieces smaller and stir into soup. If desired serve some meat in the soup and maybe serve the remaining meat sliced with mustard or horseradish next day. Sprinkle chopped parsley over soup just before serving.

COCK-A-LEEKIE

Serves 6-8

INGREDIENTS

7 cups chicken stock
6 leeks washed and sliced
Meat from 1 cooked chicken, sliced
Salt and pepper
2 tablespoons chopped parsley

METHOD

Heat chicken stock, stir in leeks and cook gently until tender. Stir in chicken and season well with salt and pepper. Simmer until piping hot, stir in parsley and serve.

Opposite page: Hearty Pea Soup with Meat, recipe above.

OXTAIL SOUP

Serves 8

INGREDIENTS

1kg (2lb) oxtail, jointed
10 cups water
Plain flour
Salt and pepper
2 tablespoons butter
125g (4oz) bacon pieces, with excess fat removed
2 onions, sliced
3 carrots, sliced
¾ cup chopped celery
2 parsley sprigs
1 bay leaf
1 thyme sprig
12 peppercorns
3 tablespoons barley
Chopped parsley

METHOD

Put the oxtail in a saucepan with the water. Bring to the boil, then simmer gently for about 2 hours. Remove the oxtail and pat dry. Chill the stock. Coat the oxtail with flour, which has been seasoned with salt and pepper.

Melt the butter and slowly fry the oxtail until browned. Add the bacon, onions, carrots, and celery and cook over gentle heat until the vegetables are browned. Remove solid fat from the stock and pour over the oxtail and vegetables. Add the parsley, bay leaf, and thyme, tied together, the peppercorns, and salt to taste. Slowly bring to the boil. Skim the surface, cover, and simmer for 1 hour.

Lift the oxtail pieces from the pan. Wash the barley and add to the pan. Remove the oxtail flesh from the bones and return to the pan. Cover and simmer for 1 hour.

Remove the bunch of herbs.

Serve sprinkled with chopped parsley.

BARLEY BROTH

Serves 8

INGREDIENTS

1kg (2lb) neck of mutton or lamb, chopped
8 cups water
125g (4oz) barley
6 cups chopped vegetables, e.g. carrot, onion, turnip
Salt and pepper

METHOD

Place neck, water and barley in a saucepan. Cover and cook gently 2 hours.

Add vegetables, salt and pepper and cook until tender. Chop meat and serve in soup.

SCOTCH BROTH

Serves 8-10

INGREDIENTS

1kg (2lb) scrag end of lamb or mutton
8 cups water
⅓ cup barley
¾ cup dried peas, soaked overnight in water
1 bay leaf
Sprig fresh thyme
Salt and pepper
2 leeks, sliced
2 large carrots, diced
1 swede or turnip, chopped
2 cups sliced cabbage

METHOD

Place meat, water, barley, drained peas, bay leaf, thyme, salt and pepper to taste in a large saucepan. Bring to boil and cook gently 2 hours. Add vegetables and simmer until tender, about ½ hour. Sprinkle with chopped parsley when serving.

JELLIED CONSOMMÉ

Serves 6-8

INGREDIENTS

1kg (2lb) mixture beef and veal bones
500g (1lb) chicken pieces
8 cups water
1 large carrot
1 large onion
Salt and peppercorns
½ cup dry sherry

METHOD

Place bones, chicken, water, whole carrot and unpeeled onion in a large saucepan.

Add salt and peppercorns to taste, cover with lid and bring to boil.

Cook gently 3 hours. Strain through a fine sieve and allow stock to cool. Stir in sherry and taste for seasoning. Chill and serve in small bowls. Use chicken in any recipe requiring cooked chicken.

gredients 500 g (1lb) firm-fleshed fish fillets 13/4 cups water 1 small cele
(4oz) scallops, split into halves 185 g (6oz) small mushrooms, thinly slic
og (8oz) prawns, shelled and deveined Buttered breadcrumbs method Re
eat the water with the celery, onion, parsley, bay leaf, and wine unti
emove the fish with a slotted spoon and put aside. Add the scallops to t
easure and reserve 11/4 cups. Cook the mushrooms and shallots gently
aped individual ovenproof dishes, or into a shallow ovenproof dish. M
e reserved fish stock and cook, stirring until boiling. Simmer for 3-4 mi
3 minutes to reheat. Spoon into the dishes or dish. Top with buttered
edium heat until crisp). Put into a hot oven to reheat.

Fish and Shellfish

stalk 1/2 small onion 2 parsley sprigs 1 bay leaf 2/3 cup dry white wine 1
shallots, finely chopped Butter Salt and pepper 1 tablespoon plain flo
ve skin from the fish and cut the flesh into small cubes, taking out bone
oiling. Simmer for 5 minutes. Add the fish and simmer until just tende
pan and simmer for 5 minutes. Remove the scallops and strain the liqui
butter until softened. Add salt and pepper to taste. Spoon into 4-6 she
1 tablespoon butter, add the flour, and stir for a minute. Gradually a
es. Add salt and pepper, then the fish, prawns, and scallops. Simmer f
umbs (about 6 tablespoons tossed in 3 tablespoons of melted butter ov

SAILORS' PIE

Serves 4

INGREDIENTS

1kg (2lb) potatoes
1 x 56g can flat anchovy fillets, drained
¼ cup grated tasty cheese
¼ cup chopped parsley
½ cup sour cream
375g (12oz) whiting or flathead fillets
Salt and pepper
250g (8oz) scallops or mussels

METHOD

Peel and cook potatoes in boiling salted water until tender. Drain. Chop anchovies and mix with cheese, parsley and sour cream.

Place fish fillets on one half of a greased ovenproof dish. Season with salt and pepper to taste and add the scallops or mussels. Cover with anchovy mixture.

Press potatoes through a sieve directly into the remaining half of the dish, next to the fish.

Bake in a moderately hot oven 20-25 minutes until fish flakes when tested with a fork and top is lightly browned.

SHELLFISH VOL-AU-VENT

Serves 4-5

INGREDIENTS

3 tablespoons butter
1 small leek, thinly sliced
125g (4oz) mushrooms, thinly sliced
3 tablespoons flour
1½ cups milk
¼ cup white wine
¼ cup cream
1 egg yolk
½ teaspoon tarragon
Salt and pepper
1 dozen oysters, shelled
1 dozen mussels, shelled
18 or 20cm (7 or 8in) vol-au-vent case
Chopped parsley
1 spring onion, finely chopped
Paprika

METHOD

Melt the butter, add the leek and mushrooms and cook gently until just softened. Sprinkle in the flour, stir a few minutes then slowly add the milk. Cook, stirring until thickened.

Stir in the wine and cook over low heat a few more minutes. Remove from heat.

Beat the cream lightly with the egg yolk and stir slowly into sauce. Add the tarragon and season with salt and pepper. Add the oysters and mussels and simmer gently 2-3 minutes.

Meanwhile heat through the pastry case in a moderate oven. Spoon the shellfish mixture into the case, garnish with parsley, spring onion and a dusting of paprika. Serve at once.

Right: Sailors' Pie, recipe above.

Bernard Hall
1859–1935
The Giant Crab (c.1928)
Oil on canvas 63.6 x 111.8cm
Felton Bequest 1930
National Gallery of Victoria,
Melbourne

LOBSTER THERMIDOR
Serves 4

INGREDIENTS
2 medium lobsters or crayfish
1¼ cups milk
1 bay leaf
½ small onion
2 cloves
3 tablespoons butter
2 tablespoons plain flour
Salt
Pinch of cayenne pepper
Pinch of grated nutmeg
4 shallots, chopped
½ cup dry white wine
1¼ cups cream
1 teaspoon French mustard
¾ cup grated Swiss cheese

METHOD
Halve the lobsters lengthwise, remove the flesh and cut into pieces, reserving the shells. Bring the milk to the boil with the bay leaf, onion, and cloves. Put aside until lukewarm and then strain. Melt half the butter, add the flour, and stir over medium heat for 1-2 minutes without letting it colour. Gradually stir in the warm milk and cook, stirring, until the sauce boils and thickens. Stir in salt to taste, cayenne pepper, and nutmeg. Simmer for 1-2 minutes. Put the lobster shells in a moderate oven to warm. Melt the remaining butter, add the shallots, and cook gently until softened. Add the wine and cook over high heat until reduced by half. Stir in the white sauce, cream, and mustard. Simmer for a minute. Stir in ½ cup of the cheese and simmer until melted. Stir in the lobster meat.

Spoon into the shells, sprinkle with the remaining cheese, and brown under the griller.

SEAFOOD À LA MODE
Serves 8

INGREDIENTS
1½ cups dry white wine
½ cup water
1 bay leaf
500g (1lb) scallops, rinsed
750g (1½lb) prawns, peeled and deveined
1 small white onion, finely chopped
2 tablespoons butter
¼ cup plain flour
½ teaspoon salt
½ cup milk
½ cup cream
8 vol-au-vent cases,
Watercress (optional)
Lemon wedges (optional)

METHOD
Bring the wine to boiling point with the water and bay leaf. Add the scallops and simmer for 3-4 minutes. Drain, reserving the liquid, and mix with the prawns.

Gently fry the onion in the butter until just tender but not browned. Stir the flour and salt in until smooth. Gradually stir in the reserved stock. Cook, stirring, until boiling. Reduce the heat and simmer for 5 minutes. Add the milk, cream, prawns, and scallops.

Stir over low heat until heated through.

Spoon into warmed pastry cases. If you wish, garnish with watercress and lemon.

Following pages: Shellfish Vol-au-vent, recipe page 28

FISH SOUFFLÉ

Serves 4

INGREDIENTS

500g (1lb) fish fillets
⅓ cup fresh breadcrumbs
2 tablespoons milk
2 eggs, separated
½ cup cream
¼ teaspoon dried tarragon
Salt
Pinch of cayenne pepper
1 teaspoon French mustard

METHOD

Remove the skin and bones and chop the fish coarsely. Put in a saucepan with the breadcrumbs, milk, lightly beaten egg yolks, and cream. Stir over gentle heat for 3-4 minutes. Remove from the heat and beat with a wooden spoon. Add the tarragon, salt to taste, cayenne pepper, and mustard. Beat again for 30 seconds. Beat the egg whites until soft peaks form and fold in.

Turn into a greased 18 cm (7 in) soufflé dish or straight-sided ovenproof dish and bake in a moderate oven for 35-40 minutes.

FISH PARISIENNE

Serves 4-6

INGREDIENTS

500g (1lb) firm-fleshed fish fillets
1¾ cups water
1 small celery stalk
½ small onion
2 parsley sprigs
1 bay leaf
⅔ cup dry white wine
125g (4oz) scallops, split into halves
185g (6oz) small mushrooms, thinly sliced
3 shallots, finely chopped
Butter
Salt and pepper
1 tablespoon plain flour
250g (8oz) prawns, shelled and deveined
Buttered breadcrumbs

METHOD

Remove skin from the fish and cut the flesh into small cubes, taking out bones. Heat the water with the celery, onion, parsley, bay leaf, and wine until boiling. Simmer for 5 minutes.

Add the fish and simmer until just tender. Remove the fish with a slotted spoon and put aside. Add the scallops to the pan and simmer for 5 minutes. Remove the scallops and strain the liquid. Measure and reserve 1¼ cups. Cook the mushrooms and shallots gently in butter until softened. Add salt and pepper to taste. Spoon into 4-6 shell-shaped individual ovenproof dishes, or into a shallow ovenproof dish.

Melt 1 tablespoon butter, add the flour, and stir for a minute. Gradually add the reserved fish stock and cook, stirring until boiling. Simmer for 3-4 minutes. Add salt and pepper, then the fish, prawns, and scallops. Simmer for 2-3 minutes to reheat.

Spoon into the dishes or dish. Top with buttered crumbs (about 6 tablespoons tossed in 3 tablespoons of melted butter over medium heat until crisp). Put into a hot oven to reheat.

MR LEE'S STIR-FRY

Serves 1-2

INGREDIENTS

Vegetable oil
1 clove garlic, crushed
2 Chinese cabbage leaves, sliced
1 carrot, cut in matchsticks
1 small turnip, cut in matchsticks
1 white onion, sliced lengthwise
4 mushrooms, sliced
2 teaspoons chopped fresh coriander or ¾ teaspoon dried
1 teaspoon finely chopped fresh ginger or ½ teaspoon ground ginger
1 tablespoon honey and 1 tablespoon lemon juice mixed with a little water
12 cooked yabbies or 6 large cooked prawns
1 tablespoon soy sauce

METHOD

Heat oil in a large heavy frypan or wok. Add garlic. Stir-fry cabbage, carrot, turnip, onion and mushrooms until lightly cooked. Add coriander, ginger, honey and lemon juice and toss quickly to blend flavours. Add yabbies or prawns and soy sauce and toss quickly to heat.

Serve with steamed rice or noodles. Multiply quantities to serve more people as you wish.

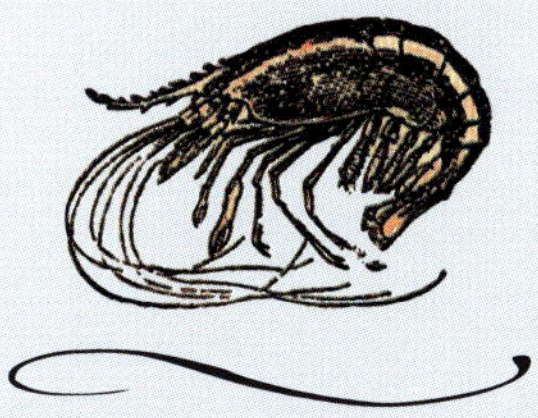

SCALLOPS MORNAY

Serves 4

INGREDIENTS

750 g (1½lb) scallops
1 cup dry white wine
60g (2oz) butter
1 small onion, chopped
3 tablespoons flour
Salt and cayenne pepper
1 cup milk
1 cup grated tasty cheese

METHOD

Cook scallops and wine gently 2-3 minutes. Remove and slice. Cook butter and onion 2-3 minutes, stir in flour, salt and pepper and cook 2 minutes.

Add milk and wine from scallops and stir until boiling and thickened. Stir in cheese and scallops. Heat through and serve.

Following pages: Mr. Lee's Stir-fry, recipe above.

x 3kg (6lb) goose 21/2 tablespoons plain flour 3 tablespoons brandy 11/2
blespoons butter 1large onion, chopped 2 Granny Smith apples, peeled,
day-old bread, toasted in the oven 2 teaspoons finely grated lemon
aspoon dried thyme Salt and pepper to taste method Make the stuffir
ith damp paper towels. Remove the oil sac from the parsonis nose, using
secure with poultry pins. Truss the bird, then wipe over with paper to
a lightly oiled baking dish. Put the dish over high heat and sear the bir
r 15 minutes. Baste, cover with foil, and reduce the temperature to mode
the cooking time. Transfer to a heated serving platter, remove the
blespoons of juice from the pan, add the remaining tablespoon of flour,
ir in the stock and cook, stirring, until boiling. Simmer for 2-3 minutes. S

Poultry

os stock made from neck and giblets of goose, or chicken stock Stuffing
ed, and diced 1 1/2 cups chopped stoned soft prunes 31/2 cups small cub
d 1/4 cup chopped parsley 1 teaspoon snipped fresh thyme leaves or 1
Remove excess fat from the inside of the goose. Wipe inside and outsi
chen scissors. Fill the cavity loosely with the stuffing. Sew up the openi
s to dry thoroughly. Sprinkle 1 1/2å tablespoons of the flour over and p
Warm the brandy, set alight, and pour over the goose. Roast in a hot ov
te. Roast for 21/2 hours, removing the foil about 30 minutes before the e
ussing string, and keep warm while you make the gravy. Pour all but
d stir over medium heat until browned, scraping up the pan juices. Slow
ve with the goose. Stuffing: Melt the butter, add the onion, and fry gent

SETTLER'S CHICKEN

Serves 4

INGREDIENTS

1 boiling fowl
5 cups water
1 carrot, sliced
2 stalks celery, sliced
1 onion or leek
2 sprigs parsley
1 onion stuck with cloves
Salt to taste

METHOD

Place all ingredients in a large saucepan, including giblets if included.

Cook with lid on over a low heat until tender about 2 hours.

Lift the fowl out and leave the stock to cook a little longer to obtain a stronger flavour.

Skim fat from top. Reserve stock for soups. Serve fowl hot, sliced with parsley sauce or cold with salad.

CHICKEN KIEV

Serves 6

INGREDIENTS

125g (4oz) butter
1 clove garlic, crushed
1 tablespoon lemon juice
2 tablespoons chopped parsley
Salt and pepper
3 whole chicken breasts, skinned, boned and halved
Flour
2 eggs, beaten
Fine dry breadcrumbs
Oil for frying

METHOD

Mix butter, garlic, lemon juice, parsley, salt and pepper together. Shape into a rectangle 5 x 8 cm (2 x 3 in). Chill until firm.

Pound chicken breasts, one piece at a time, between sheets of waxed paper until ½ cm (¼ in) thick, taking care not to tear chicken.

Cut chilled butter into 6 equal finger-sized pieces. Place in centre of chicken, fold in edges and roll up to completely enclose filling. Fasten with a wooden toothpick.

Roll in flour, then dip in beaten eggs and finally roll in the breadcrumbs. Chill 1 hour. This process may be repeated once again if desired.

Heat oil in deep fryer and cook 7-10 minutes until golden brown and completely cooked through. Drain and remove toothpicks. Serve with lightly braised cucumber slices with seeds removed and rice. Garnish with lemon wedges.

Opposite page: Settler's Chicken, recipe above

CREAMY MUSHROOM CHICKEN

Serves 4-5

INGREDIENTS

1kg (2lb) chicken pieces
12 small onions
2 tablespoons butter
125g (4oz) mushrooms, sliced
2 tablespoons flour
1 cup milk
¾ cup evaporated milk or cream
Salt and pepper
125g (4oz) bacon, cooked crisp

METHOD

Place chicken pieces, seasoned lightly with salt and pepper, in a baking dish and bake until brown and tender, about 30 minutes. Turn now and again to prevent sticking.

Cook onions until almost tender. Drain and then lightly brown in the butter. Keep hot with the chicken. Add mushrooms to the same pan in which the onions were browned, adding a little extra butter if necessary and cook until lightly browned. Remove.

Stir flour into the mushroom liquid in pan and cook 2-3 minutes. Add milk and cream and stir until thickened and boiling. Season with salt and pepper and stir in mushrooms.

Pour over chicken and onions and sprinkle with crumbled bacon. Mashed pumpkin goes well with this dish.

CURRIED FOWL

Serves 4-6

INGREDIENTS

2 tablespoons butter
1 cooking apple, peeled, cored and chopped
1 onion, chopped
1 tablespoon curry powder
1½ cups milk or water
2 tablespoons ground rice, blended with water
1 tablespoon coconut
Salt
1 cooked fowl, chopped, see Settler's Chicken, page 40

METHOD

Cook butter, apple, onion and curry powder until soft.

Stir in milk and blended ground rice and cook until thickened. Add coconut, salt and fowl and cook 15 minutes.

Opposite page: Creamy Mushroom Chicken, recipe above.

COQ AU VIN

Serves 6

INGREDIENTS

2kg (4lb) chicken pieces
2 tablespoons flour seasoned with salt and pepper
3 tablespoons butter or ghee
125g (4oz) bacon, diced
250g (8oz) very small onions
185g (6oz) button mushrooms
2 cloves garlic, crushed
½ teaspoon dried thyme
1 bay leaf
1 bottle red wine

METHOD

Roll chicken pieces in the seasoned flour. Heat butter or ghee, add chicken and brown all over. Remove from pan. Add bacon, onions and mushrooms and brown lightly. Return chicken to pan.

Stir in garlic, thyme, bay leaf and wine. Cover with tight-fitting lid and cook gently until tender, about 1½ hours.

WINE GLAZED DUCK

Serves 4

INGREDIENTS

1 large duck
Salt
Paprika
Ground ginger
1 small onion, grated
1 cup red wine
⅓ cup brown sugar
1 tablespoon cornflour
¼ teaspoon salt
2 teaspoons grated lemon rind

METHOD

Cut duck into quarters and remove any excess fat. Arrange duck pieces in a single layer in a baking dish and bake uncovered in a preheated hot oven for 30 minutes.

Remove duck from oven and pour off fat that has accumulated in the dish. Season duck pieces generously with salt, paprika and ginger and return to the dish. Sprinkle with the onion, pour in half a cup of the wine, and cover dish with a lid or aluminium foil.

Continue cooking until duck is tender (about 45 minutes) turning pieces now and then.

In a small saucepan, combine sugar, cornflour, salt, lemon rind, and remaining half cup of wine. Bring to the boil, stirring, and simmer until smooth and thickened. Spoon over duck and bake uncovered for another 10-15 minutes basting often, until duck is glazed.

W. Hardy Wilson 1881–1955
Vane's Chicken
Watercolour 33 x 37cm
purchased 1918
Art Gallery of New South Wales

GRAND VIN DE BORDEAUX
CHATEAU
NORIOU LALIBARDE
Côtes de Bourg
A. LEVRAUD

ORANGE GARLIC DUCK

Serves 4

INGREDIENTS

1 x 2.25kg (4½lb) duck
2 oranges
5 cloves garlic, crushed
Salt
Freshly ground pepper
3 tablespoons butter
1½ cups dry white wine
1 teaspoon flour
1 teaspoon butter

METHOD

Remove excess fat from inside the cavity of the duck and wipe thoroughly with a paper towel. Cut unpeeled oranges into quarters and fill into duck together with garlic, salt and pepper. Secure with small skewers.

Melt the 3 tablespoons butter in a large frying pan and brown duck all over. Remove and cook in a moderately hot oven directly on the oven grid with a baking dish underneath on the shelf below. Cook 25 minutes on each thigh side then on the back for approximately 30 minutes until tender.

When the juices start to drip into the baking dish gradually stir in the wine and baste the duck with this several times. When the duck is cooked, there should be a delicious gravy in the baking dish. Skim off excess fat. Place baking dish over direct heat and whisk in the 1 teaspoon flour and 1 teaspoon butter blended together. Stir until thickened and serve with the duck.

PHEASANT WITH APPLES

Serves 4

INGREDIENTS

4 tablespoons butter
1 x 1.5kg (3lb) pheasant, trussed
4 large Granny Smith apples, peeled, cored and sliced
2 teaspoons sugar
1¼ cups cream
1 tablespoon lemon juice
Salt and freshly ground black pepper

METHOD

Melt half the butter in a large pan. Add pheasant and brown all over. Remove.

Add remaining butter, apples and sugar and cook until soft. Place apples in an ovenproof dish, add pheasant and pour over butter mixture. Cover and bake in a moderate oven 40 minutes. Pour cream, lemon juice, salt and pepper over, replace lid and cook until tender.

Opposite page: Orange Garlic Duck, recipe above.

ROAST GOOSE

Serves 6-8

INGREDIENTS

1 x 3kg (6lb) goose
2½ tablespoons plain flour
3 tablespoons brandy
1½ cups stock made from neck and giblets of goose, or chicken stock

Stuffing
2 tablespoons butter 1 large onion, chopped
2 Granny Smith apples, peeled, cored, and diced
1½ cups chopped stoned soft prunes
3½ cups small cubes of day-old bread, toasted in the oven
2 teaspoons finely grated lemon rind
¼ cup chopped parsley
1 teaspoon snipped fresh thyme leaves or ½ teaspoon dried thyme
Salt and pepper to taste

METHOD

Make the stuffing. Remove excess fat from the inside of the goose. Wipe inside and outside with damp paper towels. Remove the oil sac from the parsonís nose, using kitchen scissors. Fill the cavity loosely with the stuffing. Sew up the opening or secure with poultry pins. Truss the bird, then wipe over with paper towels to dry thoroughly. Sprinkle 1 ½å tablespoons of the flour over and put in a lightly oiled baking dish. Put the dish over high heat and sear the bird. Warm the brandy, set alight, and pour over the goose. Roast in a hot oven for 15 minutes. Baste, cover with foil, and reduce the temperature to moderate.

Roast for 2½ hours, removing the foil about 30 minutes before the end of the cooking time.

Transfer to a heated serving platter, remove the trussing string, and keep warm while you make the gravy.

Pour all but 2 tablespoons of juice from the pan, add the remaining tablespoon of flour, and stir over medium heat until browned, scraping up the pan juices. Slowly stir in the stock and cook, stirring, until boiling. Simmer for 2-3 minutes. Serve with the goose.

Stuffing: Melt the butter, add the onion, and fry gently until softened. Add the apples and cook for 2 minutes, stirring constantly. Transfer to a bowl and mix in all remaining ingredients.

DUCK WITH FRUIT STUFFING

Serves 4

INGREDIENTS

1 x 2kg (4lb) duck
Softened butter
Juice of ½ medium lemon
½ cup orange juice
1 teaspoon gelatine
Salt and pepper

Stuffing

¾ cup chopped raisins
¼ cup chopped stoned prunes
2 medium onions, grated
1 large orange, peeled and finely chopped
Salt and pepper
2 cups soft fresh breadcrumbs
½ teaspoon dried marjoram
1 tablespoon finely grated lemon rind
1 tablespoon melted butter

METHOD

Make the stuffing and fill the duck. Close the opening with small skewers or poultry pins. Truss and put in a greased baking dish. Rub softened butter over the duck and cover loosely with foil, making sure it does not touch the bird. Bake in a moderate oven for 1 ½ hours. Remove foil and continue baking for 30 minutes, or until tender, basting occasionally with the pan juices. Remove from the dish and allow to cool before chilling in the refrigerator.

Heat the fruit juices, sprinkle the gelatine over, add salt and pepper, and stir until the gelatine has dissolved. Chill until the mixture has the consistency of unbeaten egg white. Brush over the duck and put in the refrigerator to set. Brush with the remaining fruit glaze and chill again until set.

Stuffing: Pour boiling water over the raisins and prunes. Leave for 10 minutes and then drain thoroughly. Mix the onions with the orange, salt and pepper, breadcrumbs, marjoram, lemon rind, raisins and prunes, and melted butter.

gredients 1 x 2.5kg (5lb) leg of lamb 90g (3oz) butter 1 medium onion,
hopped fresh rosemary (or 1/2 teaspoon dried) 2 teaspoons chopped fre
round pepper Gravy 11/2 tablespoons plain flour 11/2 cups stock made w
one. Heat the butter and fry onion until soft and golden. Skin and cor
rowned. Remove from heat and add breadcrumbs, herbs and salt and pep
ith string. Season with salt and pepper, arrange on a greased rack in a
bout 2 hours for well done lamb, basting now and then with juices that
arving.Gravy: Pour off all but 2 tablespoons of drippings in pan, and
ontinue stirring until gravy is smooth and thickened. Taste for seasoning
utter 1 medium onion, finely chopped 2 lamb kidneys 2 cups soft, white
aspoons chopped fresh sage (or 1/2 teaspoon dried) 2 teaspoons choppe

Meat & game

ly chopped 2 lamb kidneys 2 cups soft, white breadcrumbs 2 teaspoo
sage (or 1/2 teaspoon dried) 2 teaspoons chopped parsley Salt and fine
lamb bone method Ask the butcher to bone the lamb for you and save t
ne kidneys and cut into small dice. Add to the pan and stir until light
r to taste. Allow to cool a little, then stuff lamb and tie into a neat sha
aking dish, and place in a preheated moderate oven.Roast uncovered f
llect in the pan. Allow to rest for 20 minutes before removing string a
r in flour over low heat. When well blended, gradually stir in stock a
nd strain into a gravy boat. ingredients 1 x 2.5kg (5lb) leg of lamb 90g (30
eadcrumbs 2 teaspoons chopped fresh rosemary (or 1/2 teaspoon dried)
parsley Salt and finely ground pepper Gravy 11/2 tablespoons plain flo

SHEARERS' STEW WITH DUMPLINGS

Serves 6 hungry shearers or 8 people

INGREDIENTS

1 tablespoon oil
1 tablespoon butter
1kg (2lb) chopped mutton or two-tooth lamb, rolled in seasoned flour
3 onions, quartered
3 parsnips, thickly sliced
3 carrots, thickly sliced
2 sticks celery, chopped
Meat or vegetable stock or water
3 tablespoons chopped parsley
¾ teaspoon mixed herbs
1 tablespoon Worcestershire sauce
Salt, pepper and a pinch of sugar

METHOD

Heat oil and butter in a large heavy frypan and brown meat, adding a little extra oil if necessary. Push to one side and sauté onions until transparent. Transfer to a heavy stewpan, adding bits left in bottom of frypan blended with a little stock or water. Add parsnips, carrots and celery and sufficient stock or water to barely cover, along with parsley, herbs, Worcestershire sauce, salt, pepper and sugar. Simmer about 2 hours or until meat is tender, on low heat. Serve with Jumbuck Dumplings.

JUMBUCK DUMPLINGS

INGREDIENTS

2 cups self-raising flour
1 tablespoon chopped parsley
Salt and plenty of black pepper
About ¾ cup milk or water

METHOD

Put flour, parsley, salt and pepper in a bowl and stir in milk or water until dough forms a soft dropping consistency. With floury palms lightly roll mixture into balls and place on top of stew while it is simmering. Cover and cook, about 15 minutes before ready to serve stew.

Opposite page: Shearers' Stew with Jumbuck Dumplings, recipe above

PARSNIP CAKES

INGREDIENTS

4 medium parsnips, cooked and mashed
4 tablespoons self-raising flour
1 egg, beaten
Salt, pepper and dash of nutmeg
Butter for frying

METHOD

Mix mashed parnsips with flour, egg, salt, pepper and nutmeg. Form into cakes with floury hands and fry on both sides in butter until brown and crisp. Drain on kitchen paper.

OXTAIL STEW

Serves 4

INGREDIENTS

2 large oxtails, jointed
Plain flour
Salt and pepper
2 tablespoons oil
2 onions, sliced
1 cup water
1 cup claret
3 large tomatoes, peeled and chopped
4 cloves
4 carrots, sliced
1 cup sliced celery
1 turnip or parsnip, cubed

METHOD

Coat the oxtails with the flour seasoned with salt and pepper. Heat the oil, add the oxtails, and brown slowly all over. Add the onions and fry until softened. Pour the fat from the pan.

Add the water, claret, tomatoes, and cloves. Stir until boiling, scraping up the pan juices. Cover and simmer for 1 1/2 hours.

Cool and then chill in the refrigerator overnight. Remove the fat from the top, return to the saucepan, and add the vegetables. Cover and simmer 1 hour, or until tender.

ABERDEEN SAUSAGE

Serves 6-8

INGREDIENTS

500g (1lb) lean minced steak
250g (8oz) bacon, minced
1 cup soft breadcrumbs
Dash of tomato or Worcestershire sauce (or both)
1 teaspoon grated lemon peel
1 teaspoon mixed herbs
1 tablespoon chopped parsley
Pepper and salt
1 egg
2 hard-boiled eggs
Dry breadcrumbs

METHOD

In a bowl mix together all ingredients, except hard-boiled eggs and dry breadcrumbs.

Form into a roll. Make a pocket along centre and place hard-boiled eggs lengthwise in it.

Cover with mixture. Flour sausage well and tie in a floured cloth. Boil gently 2 hours.

While hot, carefully remove from cloth. Chill overnight. Roll in dry breadcrumbs before serving.

Serve sliced, with salads. This makes a great buffet dish.

PORK STROGANOFF

Serves 4

INGREDIENTS

750g (1½lb) pork shoulder
2 tablespoons butter
3 onions, sliced
Salt and pepper
1 cup beef stock
2 tablespoons tomato paste
1 cup sour cream
2 teaspoons soy sauce

METHOD

Cut pork into strips. Melt butter and quickly brown pork all over. Add onions, salt and pepper and cook until browned. Stir in beef stock and tomato paste. Cover with a tight-fitting lid and cook gently until tender, about 25 minutes.

Stir in sour cream and soy sauce and reheat gently. Serve with rice and crusty bread.

Following pages: Plum glazed corned beef, recipe page 59, with parsnip cakes, recipe page 54.

J. T. MORTON
LONDON
EXTRA SUPERIOR
IMPERIAL PLUMS

Frederick McCubbin
1855–1917
Girl with bird at the King Street bakery, 1886
Oil on canvas 40.7 x 46cm
purchased 1969
National Gallery of Australia, Canberra

At the time of this painting, Melbourne was a colourful, raffish city still recovering from gold mania. It had a floating population of criminals, thieves, ruffians, drunks and itinerant workers as well as a large Chinese quarter and a permanent settlement of industrious, respectable people, including about 2,000 young sewing girls and milliners' apprentices. This little girl sits on the cobbled backyard of a modest cottage in a street which is now one of the city's most dignified thoroughfares. Her meals would have been of the most basic kind reflecting her parents' British background.

On Christmas Day, if they could afford it, the family would probably sit down to a heavy meal of roast turkey or chicken, plum pudding and mince tarts, even if the temperature was unbearably hot.

PLUM GLAZED CORNED BEEF

Serves 4-8

INGREDIENTS

- 1.5kg (3lb) corned silverside
- 1 tablespoon brown sugar
- 1 tablespoon vinegar
- 1 clove garlic, sliced
- 1 onion studded with 4 cloves
- 4 peppercorns
- 1 bouquet garni (1 bay leaf, sprigs of thyme and parsley)
- 4 carrots
- 4 small onions, peeled
- 4 potatoes
- 4 medium parsnips
- 1 cup bottled plum sauce
- 1 teaspoon honey
- 1 tablespoon orange juice

METHOD

Put the corned beef in a heavy saucepan with the brown sugar, vinegar, garlic, onion with cloves, peppercorns and bouquet garni. Add enough water to cover. Heat until boiling, cover and simmer 40 minutes. Add the carrots, onions, potatoes and parsnips.

Simmer approximately 1 hour longer or until meat is tender. Remove vegetables when cooked, drain and keep warm. Reserve parsnips.

Meanwhile melt the plum sauce, honey and orange juice over hot water, blend and keep warm.

Transfer meat to a heated platter and brush with the plum glaze. Serve meat sliced and surrounded by vegetables, with Parsnip Cakes made from reserved parsnips. A green vegetable and mustard or horseradish sauce go well with this dish.

GENTLEMAN'S BREAKFAST (BUBBLE AND SQUEAK)

Serves 1

METHOD

Fry about 1 cup cubed or shredded cold corned beef in 1 tablespoon heated butter with chopped leftover vegetables, including Parsnip Cakes (about 1 cup altogether), and season with salt and pepper. Press mixture into pan and turn until browned on both sides and formed into a cake.

Place 1 fried egg on top. Sprinkle with chopped parsley and serve with a selection of bottled sauces.

Cooked cold cabbage and potatoes may be fried with corned beef instead of leftover vegetables, as in the Irish dish called Colcannon or as it is known in England, Bubble and Squeak.

Following pages: Gentleman's Breakfast, is a version of Bubble and Squeak, and is made from cold Plum Glazed Corned Beef, leftover vegetables and Parsnip Cakes, recipes. Recipe above.

17, 1854.
MISCELLANEOUS.
No. 1.—Vol. I.
LIST OF AGENTS.

Stanley Rogers & Son

PORK MADEIRA

Serves 6

INGREDIENTS

1kg (2lb) pork fillets
2 tablespoons flour
Salt
Freshly ground pepper
2 tablespoons vegetable oil
1 tablespoon butter
1 onion, chopped
375g (12oz) button mushrooms
2 tablespoons butter, extra
½ cup unsweetened apple juice
½ cup thickened cream
½ cup Madeira
1 tablespoon tomato paste

METHOD

Cut pork into thick pieces and toss in the flour, seasoned with salt and pepper.

Heat oil and 1 tablespoon of butter together, add onion and cook slowly until just changing colour. Stir in mushrooms and cook a few more minutes. Remove onion and mushrooms from pan.

Heat the extra butter, add pork and cook quickly 7-10 minutes. Stir in onion and mushrooms and cook for 1 minute.

Add apple juice, cream, Madeira and tomato paste and stir until thickened and very hot.

Serve with rice or potatoes and salad.

BLANQUETTE DE VEAU

Serves 4

INGREDIENTS

1kg (2lb) diced veal
1 onion, studded with 4 whole cloves
1 strip lemon peel
2 cloves garlic, crushed
½ cup sliced celery
1 carrot, sliced
1 bay leaf
2 cups dry white wine
½ cup cream
2 tablespoons dry vermouth

METHOD

Place meat in a saucepan, add onion studded with the cloves, lemon peel, garlic, celery, carrot, bay leaf and wine. Cover and simmer until tender, about 1 hour.

Remove meat from stock, remove cloves and purÈe stock and vegetables together. Taste for seasoning and return to saucepan. Stir in cream and vermouth and cook until required thickness.

Return meat to sauce and heat through gently. Serve with creamy mashed potato or hot boiled rice.

PORK CHOPS WITH APPLES

Serves 4

INGREDIENTS

4 pork loin chops Salt and pepper
1 tablespoon fresh thyme
2 tablespoons apple cider
4 apples
1 cup apple cider
Salt and pepper
½ cup whipped cream

METHOD

Make several cuts in the fat around edge of chops. Cook in a frypan until brown on both sides, adding a little oil only if necessary. Season with salt, pepper and thyme.
Pour over the 2 tablespoons cider.

Peel, halve and core apples. Poach for a few minutes in the 1 cup of cider. Make cuts in 4 of the apple halves 5 mm (¼ in) apart, taking care not to cut right through.

Remove chops from pan and place in a heatproof dish. Place a sliced apple half on top.

Cut the remaining apples in chunks and purÈe in a blender with the apple cooking liquid and any liquid or scrapings from the frypan. Season with salt and pepper. Pour around the chops.

Spoon some whipped cream over the apples and grill under a medium heat until apples begin to brown.

MELBOURNE GRILL

Serves 4

INGREDIENTS

4 bacon rashers
4 lamb loin chops, trimmed
4 thick slices fillet, or Scotch fillet or small pieces rump steak
4 sausages, parboiled
2 large firm tomatoes, halved crosswise
Melted butter
4 lamb kidneys, skinned and halved
8 large mushrooms
Salt and freshly ground pepper

METHOD

Fry bacon, chops, steaks, sausages and tomatoes on grill and cook until brown.

Turn over, add kidneys with cores removed and mushrooms brushed with melted butter.

Turn kidneys after 2 minutes. When cooked, season with salt and pepper and serve on heated plates.

Chops and steaks can be topped with butter. Serve with chips or mashed potato, green vegetable or salad.

RICH CASSEROLE OF BEEF

Serves 4

INGREDIENTS

750g (1½lb) chuck steak, cubed
2 tablespoons plain flour
Salt and pepper
2-3 tablespoons oil
1 cup red wine
1 bay leaf
1 teaspoon fresh thyme
1 clove garlic, crushed
2 tablespoons tomato paste
1 teaspoon juniper berries, optional
12 small onions
2 carrots, sliced
1 stalk celery, sliced
1 leek, sliced

METHOD

Toss meat in the flour seasoned with salt and pepper and coat evenly. Brown in the hot oil all over and transfer to an ovenproof dish.

Stir wine into the pan, scraping well to mix in any flour or brown pieces left in the bottom. Add bay leaf, thyme, garlic, tomato paste and juniper berries. Mix well and pour over meat. Cover with lid and cook gently in a moderate oven 1 hour. Add onions, carrots and celery and cook another 30 minutes. Add leeks and cook until meat is tender, about 20-30 minutes.

PIG'S TROTTERS IN RED WINE

Serves 4

INGREDIENTS

6-8 pig's trotters
Salt and freshy ground black pepper
2 tablespoons butter
1 leek, washed and sliced
1 cup sliced celery
1 cup sliced carrot
1 onion, studded with 4 whole cloves
1½ cups red wine
3 cloves garlic, crushed
2 tomatoes, peeled and sliced
1 teaspoon fresh thyme
1 teaspoon fresh rosemary
1 teaspoon fresh tarragon

METHOD

Season meat with the salt and pepper and brown all over in the butter. Add leek, celery, carrot and the onion studded with the cloves. SautÈ for a few minutes.

Pour over the wine, add garlic, sliced tomato, thyme, rosemary and tarragon. Bring to the boil, cover with lid and cook until tender, about 1½ hours.

Opposite page: Rich Casserole of Beef, recipe above.

COLONIAL GOOSE

Serves 6

INGREDIENTS

1 x 2.5kg (5lb) leg of lamb
90g (3oz) butter
1 medium onion, finely chopped
2 lamb kidneys
2 cups soft, white breadcrumbs
2 teaspoons chopped fresh rosemary (or ½ teaspoon dried)
2 teaspoons chopped fresh sage (or ½ teaspoon dried)
2 teaspoons chopped parsley
Salt and finely ground pepper

Gravy

1½ tablespoons plain flour
1½ cups stock made with lamb bone

METHOD

Ask the butcher to bone the lamb for you and save the bone. Heat the butter and fry onion until soft and golden. Skin and core the kidneys and cut into small dice. Add to the pan and stir until lightly browned. Remove from heat and add breadcrumbs, herbs and salt and pepper to taste. Allow to cool a little, then stuff lamb and tie into a neat shape with string. Season with salt and pepper, arrange on a greased rack in a baking dish, and place in a preheated moderate oven.

Roast uncovered for about 2 hours for well done lamb, basting now and then with juices that collect in the pan. Allow to rest for 20 minutes before removing string and carving.

Gravy: Pour off all but 2 tablespoons of drippings in pan, and stir in flour over low heat. When well blended, gradually stir in stock and continue stirring until gravy is smooth and thickened. Taste for seasoning and strain into a gravy boat.

IRISH STEW

Serves 6

INGREDIENTS

1kg (2lb) lamb stewing chops
1.5kg (3lb) potatoes, peeled
500g (1lb) onions, sliced thickly
Salt and pepper
2½ cups water

METHOD

Trim chops. Slice ¼ of the potatoes and halve the rest. Place sliced potatoes in a deep saucepan, add chops then the potato halves.

Season with salt and pepper and pour over the water. Cover with a tight-fitting lid and cook gently for about 2 hours until chops are tender.

SAVOURY BEEF OLIVES

Serves 4-5

INGREDIENTS

500g (1lb) very thin sliced beef (4 slices)
½ cup soft breadcrumbs
2 tablespoons chopped parsley
1 small apple, peeled and chopped
1 bacon rasher, chopped
½ teaspoon dried mixed herbs
Salt and pepper
2 tablespoons seasoned flour
2 tablespoons vegetable oil
2 large carrots, sliced
1 large onion, sliced
1½ cups beef stock
2 tablespoons tomato paste
1 bay leaf

METHOD

Trim steak if necessary and cut into 10 cm (4 in) squares. Combine breadcrumbs, parsley, apple, bacon, herbs, salt and pepper to taste. Divide between the meat slices, roll up and secure with strong cotton. Roll in the seasoned flour.

Heat the oil and brown meat rolls all over. Place in a greased ovenproof dish together with carrots and onion and sprinkle over any remaining flour.

Mix together beef stock and tomato paste. Add bay leaf and pour into dish. Cover and bake in a moderately slow oven 1-1¼ hours until tender. Remove cotton before serving.

HAM FLORENTINE

Serves 4

INGREDIENTS

1 bunch spinach
½ teaspoon nutmeg
4 ham steaks
1½ cups grated tasty cheese
1 cup evaporated milk
½ cup milk
2 teaspoons cornflour

METHOD

Wash spinach leaves thoroughly under cold running water. Cook in a small amount of boiling salted water until tender, about 10 minutes. Drain and press out as much liquid as possible.

Place spinach in a greased ovenproof dish and sprinkle with the nutmeg. Add the ham steaks cut in half.

Place cheese and milks in a saucepan and stir over a low heat until cheese melts.

Blend cornflour with a little cold water, stir into cheese mixture and simmer 2-3 minutes.

Pour over ham and bake in a hot oven 20-25 minutes.

W. B. McInnes
Still Life, [date unknown]
Oil on canvas 43.3 x 58.5cm
Gift of Mr A.H. Batwell and Mrs
V.A. Ure Smith 1946
Art Gallery of New South Wales

RABBIT CASSEROLE

Serves 4

INGREDIENTS

1 rabbit, cut into serving pieces
2 teaspoons vinegar
Plain flour seasoned with salt and pepper
1 tablespoon oil
1 tablespoon butter
3 medium onions, coarsely chopped
3 rashers streaky bacon, diced
1 tablespoon plain flour
1 cup dry white wine
½ cup chicken stock
1 tablespoon tomato paste
2 sprigs parsley
1 sprig thyme
1 bay leaf
Salt and freshly ground pepper
125g (4oz) button mushrooms, halved or sliced
1 tablespoon extra butter
Chopped parsley to garnish

METHOD

Soak rabbit for 6–8 hours in cold salted water with the vinegar added. Drain pieces and dry thoroughly, then coat with seasoned flour.

Heat together oil and butter, add the rabbit pieces and brown all over. Transfer rabbit to an ovenproof dish. Add onions and bacon to the pan and gently fry until onions have softened. Add the flour, stir for a minute or two, then pour in the wine and chicken stock. Add the tomato paste and stir until boiling. Pour over rabbit in dish, add the parsley, thyme and bay leaf, tied together, with salt and pepper to taste.

Cover and cook in a moderately slow oven for about 1½ hours, or until tender. Just before cooking time is finished, quickly fry the mushrooms in extra butter for a minute or two and mix into the casserole. Remove bundle of herbs and serve casserole garnished with chopped parsley.

eggs, separated 1/2 cup caster sugar 1 cup milk, heated 3 teaspoons ge
emon Sauce 1 egg yolk 1/4 cup sugar 60 g (2oz) butter, softened 2 teaspoo
nd sugar together. Add hot milk and stir thoroughly. Pour into a sauc
elatine and stir until dissolved. Pour into a bowl and stir over chilled wa
ntil thick. Fold both into orange mixture until evenly mixed. Pour into
avoured with orange brandy liqueur and chilled thoroughly, and lemon

Puddings

ne, softened in a little water 1 cup orange juice 1 x 300 ml carton crea
cornflour 1/2 cup orange juice 1/4 cup lemon juice method Beat egg yol
an and stir over a low heat until hot and almost boiling. Add soften
until cold. Stir in orange juice. Beat egg whites until stiff and whip crea
glass serving dish and chill thoroughly. Serve with peeled orange slic
ce. Lemon sauce: Place all ingredients in a saucepan and whisk togeth

LIQUEUR SOUFFLÈ

Serves 6

INGREDIENTS

⅓ cup caster sugar
1½ tablespoons plain flour
¾ cup milk
¼ cup Orange CuraÁao
1 tablespoon butter
5 egg yolks, beaten
7 egg whites
Pinch salt

METHOD

Stir sugar and flour together in a saucepan. Gradually add milk and stir over a low heat until boiling and thickened.

Remove from heat, stir in liqueur and butter. Pour a little of the hot mixture onto the beaten yolks, stirring well. Return all to saucepan and beat until evenly mixed.

Beat egg whites with a pinch of salt until thick and gently fold into yolk mixture. Pour into a greased (and lightly sprinkled with sugar) 6-cup soufflÈ dish.

Bake in a moderately hot oven 35-40 minutes until outside is firm and inside creamy. Serve immediately with top sprinkled with sifted icing sugar.

PEARS BELLE HÈLËNE

Serves 4

INGREDIENTS

2 cups water
¾ cup sugar
Strip of orange rind, with pith removed
4 medium, firm pears

Chocolate Sauce

⅔ cup water
2 tablespoons sugar
90g (3oz) plain dark chocolate, chopped

METHOD

Heat the water with the sugar, stirring until the sugar has dissolved. Simmer until syrupy and add the orange rind. Peel the pears and core from the base (leave the stalks on).

Add the pears to the syrup, cover, and cook gently until just tender. Leave in the syrup until cold. Drain the pears thoroughly, stand each upright in an individual bowl, or on a serving plate, and spoon some of the chocolate sauce over each.

Chocolate sauce: Put the water and sugar in a saucepan and heat, stirring until the sugar has dissolved. Simmer the syrup for 3-4 minutes. Put the chocolate in a bowl and melt over a saucepan of hot water, stirring occasionally. Pour off the water from the saucepan and add the melted chocolate. Beat in the syrup, a little at a time, using a wooden spoon.

Simmer, stirring, until a thick syrup forms.

Opposite page: Liqueur Souffle, recipe above.

QUEEN OF PUDDINGS

Serves 6-8

INGREDIENTS

1 cup soft, white breadcrumbs
2 cups milk, scalded
2 eggs, separated
⅓ cup sugar
3 tablespoons strawberry jam
1 cup sliced strawberries

METHOD

Place breadcrumbs in a bowl with hot milk and let stand for 10 minutes. Beat egg yolks with half the sugar and stir into crumb mixture.

Spoon custard into a greased ovenproof dish and bake in a moderately slow oven for 45 minutes, or until firm to the touch.

Combine strawberry jam and sliced strawberries and spread over custard. Whip egg whites until stiff, then beat in remaining sugar to form a meringue.

Swirl meringue over top. Increase oven temperature to moderately hot, and bake pudding for 8-10 minutes, or until meringue is set and lightly browned. Serve hot or warm, by itself or with pouring cream.

SAGO PLUM PUDDING

Serves 4

INGREDIENTS

½ cup sago
1 cup milk
1 cup soft breadcrumbs
1 cup raisins
½ cup sugar
¼ teaspoon bicarbonate of soda
2 tablespoons butter, melted
A little extra milk, if needed

Sweet White Sauce (recipe follows)

METHOD

Place sago and milk in a large bowl and soak overnight.

Mix in remaining ingredients, adding a little more milk if necessary, to a dropping consistency.

Turn mixture into a greased 6-cup basin, cover with lid or greased foil and steam for 3 hours.

Unmould on to a serving plate and serve with Sweet White Sauce.

Sweet white sauce: Mix 3 teaspoons cornflour, pinch of salt, 1 tablespoon sugar and 1 tablespoon melted butter in a saucepan. Add 1 cup milk little by little, stirring until smoothly blended. Place over moderate heat and stir constantly until boiling. Simmer very gently for 5 minutes, then add 1 teaspoon of vanilla essence. Serve hot.

OLD ENGLISH TRIFLE

Serves 6

INGREDIENTS

1 x 20 cm (8 in) sponge cake
Apricot or raspberry jam
½ cup sherry
¼ cup brandy
2½ cups vanilla custard
½ cup toasted chopped almonds
Whipped cream
Strawberries

METHOD

Slice cake and spread with jam. Place in a glass dish. Pour over sherry, brandy and lastly custard and chill thoroughly. Sprinkle toasted almonds on top and decorate with cream and strawberries.

PEARS IN CLARET

Serves 4

INGREDIENTS

2 cups claret
1 tablespoon lemon juice
1 tablespoon orange juice
¼ cup sugar
1 stick cinnamon
4 pears

METHOD

Place claret, lemon juice, orange juice, sugar and cinnamon in a saucepan and heat gently.

Peel pears without removing stems and add to wine syrup.

Cook gently until pears are soft when tested with the point of a sharp knife.

Reduce liquid if necessary after removing pears. Replace pears and leave until cooled.

Serve with whipped cream.

ORANGE SNOW WITH LEMON SAUCE

Serves 8-10

INGREDIENTS

3 eggs, separated
½ cup caster sugar
1 cup milk, heated
3 teaspoons gelatine, softened in a little water
1 cup orange juice
1 x 300ml carton cream

Lemon Sauce
1 egg yolk
¼ cup sugar
60g (2oz) butter, softened
2 teaspoons cornflour
½ cup orange juice
¼ cup lemon juice

METHOD

Beat egg yolks and sugar together. Add hot milk and stir thoroughly. Pour into a saucepan and stir over a low heat until hot and almost boiling. Add softened gelatine and stir until dissolved.

Pour into a bowl and stir over chilled water until cold. Stir in orange juice. Beat egg whites until stiff and whip cream until thick. Fold both into orange mixture until evenly mixed.

Pour into a glass serving dish and chill thoroughly. Serve with peeled orange slices flavoured with orange brandy liqueur and chilled thoroughly, and lemon sauce.

Lemon sauce: Place all ingredients in a saucepan and whisk together thoroughly.

Stir over a low heat until thickened and boiling. Stir over chilled water until cold. If sauce thickens too much for pouring, thin down with a little cream.

LEMON SHERRY MOULD

Serves 4-5

INGREDIENTS

1 tablespoon gelatine
¼ cup lemon juice
3 egg whites
¾ cup caster sugar
¾ cup cream, whipped
Grated rind 1 lemon
¼ cup sherry

METHOD

Soften gelatine in the lemon juice in a heatproof cup and stir over hot water until dissolved.

Cool until just starting to thicken.

Beat egg whites until thick, gradually add sugar and beat until thick like meringue.

Fold in whipped cream, lemon rind, sherry and gelatine mixture.

Pour into a wet or lightly oiled 5-cup mould and chill overnight. Unmould onto a serving plate and top and surround with berries or seedless grapes.

Opposite page: Orange Snow with Lemon Sauce, recipe above.

APPLES MARZIPAN

Serves 4-5

INGREDIENTS

4 cooking apples
½ cup water
¼ cup sugar
1 x 200g roll marzipan, grated
2 eggs

METHOD

Peel, core and cut apples into wedges. Stir water and sugar together over a low heat until boiling. Add apples, cover with tight-fitting lid and cook 5-7 minutes, until still slightly firm.

Drain and place in a greased ovenproof dish.

Beat grated marzipan and eggs together in an electric mixer until thick and creamy. Pour over apples and bake in a hot oven 20 minutes until golden brown.

Serve with custard or ice-cream.

BREAD AND BUTTER CUSTARD

Serves 4-5

INGREDIENTS

4-5 slices white bread
Butter
½ cup sultanas
3 eggs
2 cups milk
2 tablespoons sugar
1 teaspoon vanilla essence
Nutmeg

METHOD

Spread the bread with butter and either leave whole or cut into fingers.

Place sultanas in a greased ovenproof dish and cover with bread.

Beat eggs, milk, sugar and vanilla together and pour over bread. Allow to stand 20 minutes.

Sprinkle with nutmeg and bake in a moderate oven 35-40 minutes.

Serve warm with apple sauce.

Hugh Ramsay
1877–1906
Portrait of Miss Nellie Patterson c.1903
Oil on canvas 122.3 x 92.2cm
National Gallery of Australia, Canberra

This little girl was born at the end of the 19th century into an affluent family as the Australian colony developed and prospered. Her portrait was painted two years after Federation, presenting her in an atmosphere of luxurious comfort and as a pampered and adored child dressed for a party in ruffles and frills with a satin sash. Perhaps it was her own birthday party, no doubt a lavish event with an elaborate spread of jellies, cakes, jam tarts and home made lemonade. Although she lived in a faraway country, her life would have been circumscribed by English town and country manners and customs, with nannies and nursery teas, pony rides and pets, an adopted rarified lifestyle reserved only for a special few settlers.

APRICOT RICE CREAM

Serves 5

INGREDIENTS

⅔ cup rice
2¾ cups milk
½ teaspoon vanilla essence
⅓ cup sugar
1 x 822g (26oz) can apricot halves
1 cup cream, whipped
1 egg white
Toasted almond slivers
Extra cream (optional)

METHOD

Pour 1 cup boiling water over rice, leave for 10 minutes and then drain.

Put rice into a saucepan, add milk and vanilla and cook gently, stirring occasionally, until rice is tender. Add sugar, stir until dissolved, put aside until cold.

Drain apricots, take out a third, chop into small pieces and fold into the rice, with the cream.

Beat egg white until stiff, fold in.

Turn into a serving bowl and chill. To serve, decorate with apricot halves, almond slivers and whipped cream.

Note: *If you wish, omit cream from top and serve the sweet with apricot sauce. For the sauce, put ¾ cup canned apricot nectar into a saucepan, add 1 tablespoon brandy and heat. Mix 2 teaspoons arrowroot or cornflour to a paste with a little water, add to pan and stir until boiling. Add a pinch of cinnamon, serve when cold.*

ICE CREAM ROMANOFF

Serves 2

INGREDIENTS

4 peach halves, sliced
12 strawberries
Vanilla ice-cream
Green peppermint liqueur

METHOD

Arrange fruit in 2 parfait glasses. Top with ice-cream and pour over the liqueur.

SWEET RUM OMELETTE

Serves 4

INGREDIENTS

4 eggs, separated
4 tablespoons caster sugar
1 tablespoon butter

Sauce
(recipe follows)

METHOD

Preheat the griller to moderate. Beat egg yolks with 2 tablespoons of sugar until creamy.

Beat egg whites until stiff, gradually beat in rest of sugar and fold into the yolks.

Melt butter in a 20 cm (8 in) omelette pan, pour in mixture and cook over moderate heat 5-7 minutes, lifting side with spatula to test when underneath is golden.

Put omelette, in the pan, under the griller for a few minutes, or until top is firm and golden.

Fold in half, turn on to a warm serving dish, pour the sauce over and serve with vanilla ice-cream.

Sauce: Melt 125 g (4 oz) butter with 2 tablespoons caster sugar and grated rind of 1 medium-sized orange. When sugar has dissolved, add ¼ cup of rum, heat well, then set alight and pour over omelette.

ROLY POLY PUDDING

Serves 4-5

INGREDIENTS

1½ cups self-raising flour
125g (4oz) butter
1 tablespoon caster sugar
¼ cup mixture milk and water
½ cup loosely packed brown sugar
1 teaspoon ground ginger
½ teaspoon mixed spice
½ cup sultanas
½ cup currants
¼ cup chopped mixed peel

METHOD

Sift flour, rub in butter until mixture resembles fine breadcrumbs, mix in caster sugar.

Stir in enough of the milk and water to form a firm dough.

Knead lightly on a floured surface until smooth, roll out thinly to a rectangle. Mix together brown sugar and spices, sprinkle over pastry to 2.5 cm (1 in) from edges.

Sprinkle the sultanas, currants and peel over, brush edges with milk. Roll up as for a Swiss roll from the long edge, seal ends.

Lift on to a greased oven tray, brush over with milk and sprinkle with sugar. Bake in a moderately hot oven 25-30 minutes, or until golden brown.

CRËME CARAMEL

Serves 6

INGREDIENTS

1 cup caster sugar
½ cup water
1½ cups milk
½ cup cream
⅓ cup sugar
4 eggs, beaten
1 teaspoon vanilla essence

METHOD

Place caster sugar and water in a small saucepan and stir over a low heat until sugar dissolves. Cook without stirring until golden brown and remove from heat immediately.

Take care not to burn.

Pour quickly into 6 individual greased moulds and rotate to coat the sides.

Heat milk and cream together. Add the ⅓ cup sugar and stir until dissolved. Cool to lukewarm. Pour onto beaten eggs and vanilla and mix well.

Pour into caramel lined moulds and place in a baking tin half filled with warm water.

Bake in a moderate oven 20-25 minutes until set. Remove from water and allow to cool.

Chill in refrigerator overnight. Run a knife carefully around sides if unmoulding, otherwise serve straight from dishes.

DUCHESS OF YORK PUDDING

Serves 4

INGREDIENTS

60g (2oz) butter
¼ cup sugar
2 eggs
1 cup self raising flour
2 tablespoons raspberry jam or marmalade
½ teaspoon bicarbonate of soda

METHOD

Beat butter and sugar until soft and creamy. Beat in eggs. Mix in flour, jam and bicarbonate of soda. Place in a greased pudding basin and cover with buttered paper.

Tie securely, place in a saucepan half filled with boiling water and allow to cook gently 1½ hours. Serve hot with custard.

Opposite page: Creme Caramel, recipe above.

Fine
Calvados Boul

LE GRAND MARNIER
est à Base de Cognac

ORANGE CRÉPES

Serves 8-9

INGREDIENTS

Crépes:

1 cup plain flour
Pinch salt
1 egg
1¼ cups milk
1 tablespoon butter, melted

Filling:

250g (8oz) packaged cream cheese
3 tablespoons sour cream
Grated rind 1 orange

Sauce:

60g (2oz) butter
¼ cup orange juice
3 tablespoons icing sugar
Grated rind 1 lemon
1 tablespoon lemon juice
½ cup orange brandy liqueur
½ cup brandy

METHOD

Sift flour and salt into a basin. Add egg and gradually stir in milk, beating until smooth. Stir in melted butter.

Heat a crépe pan, brush with melted butter, pour in ¼ cup batter, tilt pan to cover base completely and cook quickly on both sides. Repeat until all the batter is used.

Beat cream cheese, sour cream and orange rind together until creamy and spread on each crépe. Fold into 4 and place close together in a chafing dish.

Melt butter, stir in orange juice, icing sugar, lemon rind and juice and stir well. Add liqueur and heat thoroughly. Pour over crépes and re-heat, spooning sauce over crépes all the time.

Pour over warmed brandy and shake gently to spread it over crépes.

Ignite and serve flaming.

Left: Orange Crepes, recipe above.

:up caster sugar 11/2 tablespoons butter 21/2 tablespoons cocoa 4 table
'eam filling: 1 cup cream 1 tablespoon cocoa, sifted 1 tablespoon caste
fted 1 tablespoon water Few drops of vanilla essence method Beat the e
ntinue beating for about 15 minutes or until very thick and creamy. A
ld into the egg mixture. Sift the flour and salt twice, sift again over th
in) sandwich tins and bake in a moderate oven for 20-25 minutes, or un
e fingertip and the cakes are beginning to shrink from the sides of the
til cold. Split each layer of cake in half. Join the layers together with t
e surface with a spatula dipped in very hot water. Decorate with waln

Cakes, Pies and Breads

ons boiling water 11/4 cups self-raising flour Pinch of salt Walnut halv
igar Chocolate glacé icing: 1 cup icing sugar, sifted 2 tablespoons coco
until the yolks and whites are combined. Gradually beat in the sugar ar
the butter and cocoa to the boiling water, stir until combined, and the
ixture, and fold in lightly and evenly. Divide between two greased 20 c
the tops of the cakes spring back immediately when touched lightly wi
s. Invert the cakes carefully on to a wire rack, remove the tins, and lea
cream filling. Pour the glacé icing over immediately. If necessary, smoo
halves. Cream filling: Put the cream in a bowl and sprinkle the cocoa ar

APPLE-MARMALADE PIE

Serves 8

INGREDIENTS

1½ cups flour
Pinch salt
155g (5oz) butter
2 tablespoons hot water
1kg (2lb) Granny Smith apples, peeled and sliced
3 tablespoons marmalade
2-3 cloves
½ cup caster sugar
Unbeaten egg white
Extra sugar
Ground cinnamon

METHOD

Sift flour and salt, add the butter melted in the hot water and blend, adding flour or more hot water until mixture is a workable consistency. Roll out lightly on a floured board and line a 23 cm (9 in) springform cake tin.

Mix together the sliced apples, marmalade, cloves and sugar and place in the pastry case.

Brush edges with hot water and cover with remaining pastry, pressing edges together to seal. Decorate with pastry trimmings and make a vent in the centre for steam to escape.

Brush with unbeaten egg white, sprinkle generously with sugar and bake in a moderately hot oven 40-50 minutes until pastry is golden brown. Cover with foil if pastry is browning too much.

When ready to serve, dust with cinnamon. Serve hot or cold with whipped sweetened cream flavoured with cinnamon.

GEM SCONES

Makes 12-16

INGREDIENTS

1½ tablespoons softened butter
2 tablespoons sugar
1 egg
½ cup milk
1 cup self-raising flour
Pinch of salt

METHOD

Beat the butter with the sugar until creamy. Add the egg and beat well. Stir in the milk.

Sift together the flour and salt and fold in. Spoon into very hot, greased gem irons, filling to ¾. Bake in a hot oven for 10–15 minutes.

Opposite page: Apple-Marmalade Pie.

COCKATOO
HIGH
GRADE

Lemon Syrup

LITTLE LEMON TARTS

Makes 20

INGREDIENTS

1¼ cups plain flour
½ teaspoon salt
2 tablespoons caster sugar
125g (4oz) butter
1 egg yolk
1 tablespoon lemon juice

Lemon Butter:
125g (4oz) butter
1 cup sugar
Finely grated rind of 3 medium lemons
½ cup lemon juice
4 eggs, lightly beaten

METHOD

Sift dry ingredients together. Add the butter and rub in until the mixture resembles fine bread crumbs. Mix the egg yolk with the lemon juice and add to the flour. Mix together and knead gently to form a smooth ball. Wrap and chill for 30 minutes. Roll out on a floured surface and cut in circles to line fluted tartlet tins. Bake in a moderate oven 12-15 minutes or until light golden. Remove from tins and leave until cold. Fill with lemon butter. Serve with whipped cream.

Lemon butter: Melt the butter over hot water. Add the sugar and stir until dissolved. Mix in the lemon rind and juice. Quickly stir in the eggs. Stir over boiling water until mixture is thick enough to coat the back of a wooden spoon - about 5 minutes. Strain, pour into hot sterilised jars, and seal. When cold store in the refrigerator until needed.

PRESERVED LEMONS

INGREDIENTS

12 fresh lemons
Boiling water
Sugar

METHOD

Place lemons in a large saucepan and pour over boiling water to just cover. Cook gently until almost tender. Remove with a slotted spoon.

Measure liquid and add 2 cups sugar to 1½ cups liquid. Boil these two ingredients together for 5 minutes. Pierce lemons with a skewer, add to syrup and cook until softened. Place in wide-necked jars, cover with syrup, seal and leave 2 weeks before using.

Delicious served chilled and sliced with ice-cream for an unusual dessert.

Opposite page: Sydney's north-west was the first area producing citrus fruits. Oranges and lemons were popular and used for delicacies such as Little Lemon Tarts, as well as Preserved Lemons, recipes above and Lemon Syrup, recipe page 93.

CINNAMON TEA CAKE

INGREDIENTS

1 cup self-raising flour
½ teaspoon cinnamon
¼ teaspoon nutmeg
1 egg, separated
½ cup sugar
½ cup milk
Vanilla essence
1½ tablespoons butter, melted
Extra melted butter
1 teaspoon cinnamon
1 tablespoon sugar

METHOD

Sift the flour with the ½ teaspoon of cinnamon and the nutmeg. Beat the egg white until stiff. Add the egg yolk and mix in. Gradually beat in the ½ cup of sugar. Slowly stir in the milk and vanilla essence. Stir in the sifted dry ingredients, with the melted butter.

Spoon into a greased 18 cm (7 in) round sandwich tin and bake in a moderate oven for 30 minutes. While still hot, brush the top with extra melted butter and sprinkle with the teaspoon of cinnamon mixed with the tablespoon of sugar.

Serve warm or cold, with butter.

CHEESE STRAWS

Makes 70

INGREDIENTS

½ cup plain flour
½ cup self-raising flour
½ teaspoon salt
¼ teaspoon paprika
Pinch of cayenne pepper
1½ cups grated matured Cheddar cheese
1 egg
¼ cup beer
Extra beer
Sesame seeds or coarse salt

METHOD

Sift the flours into a mixing bowl with the salt, paprika, and cayenne pepper. Stir in the cheese. Beat the egg lightly and stir in the beer. Pour over the flour and mix to a firm dough.

Knead lightly on a floured surface, then roll out thinly and cut into 10 x 1 cm (4 x 1/2 in) strips. Arrange on an ungreased oven tray, brush lightly with beer, and sprinkle with sesame seeds or salt. Bake in a moderate oven for 15-20 minutes.

LAYERED CHOCOLATE SPONGE

INGREDIENTS

4 eggs
1 cup caster sugar
1½ tablespoons butter
2½ tablespoons cocoa
4 tablespoons boiling water
1¼ cups self-raising flour
Pinch of salt
Walnut halves

Cream filling:
1 cup cream
1 tablespoon cocoa, sifted
1 tablespoon caster sugar

Chocolate glacé icing:
1 cup icing sugar, sifted
2 tablespoons cocoa, sifted
1 tablespoon water
Few drops of vanilla essence

METHOD

Beat the eggs until the yolks and whites are combined. Gradually beat in the sugar and continue beating for about 15 minutes or until very thick and creamy. Add the butter and cocoa to the boiling water, stir until combined, and then fold into the egg mixture.

Sift the flour and salt twice, sift again over the mixture, and fold in lightly and evenly. Divide between two greased 20 cm (8 in) sandwich tins and bake in a moderate oven for 20-25 minutes, or until the tops of the cakes spring back immediately when touched lightly with the fingertip and the cakes are beginning to shrink from the sides of the tins.

Invert the cakes carefully on to a wire rack, remove the tins, and leave until cold. Split each layer of cake in half. Join the layers together with the cream filling. Pour the glacé icing over immediately. If necessary, smooth the surface with a spatula dipped in very hot water. Decorate with walnut halves.

Cream filling: Put the cream in a bowl and sprinkle the cocoa and sugar over. Chill for at least 30 minutes. Whip until thick.

Chocolate glacé icing: Sift the icing sugar and cocoa together and put in a saucepan with the water and vanilla essence. Heat very carefully, stirring, until the mixture is of a pouring consistency.

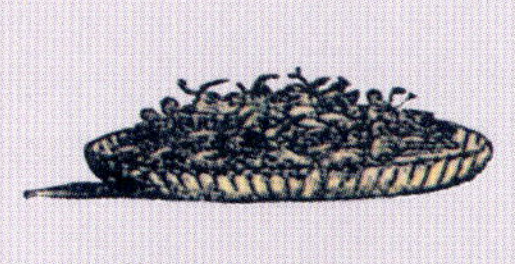

Following pages: Many of the new arrivals who came from Britain and Europe to populate Australia brought their favourite family "receipts" with them. These recipes have been absorbed into our gastronomic culture. One of the most popular from Scotland was the sweet crumbly buttery biscuit-like cake called shortbread, recipe above, which is traditionally cut or broken into segments at the table.

LEMON SYRUP

INGREDIENTS

3½ cups freshly squeezed lemon juice
4 cups sugar
2 teaspoons citric acid
2 teaspoons tartaric acid
2 teaspoons epsom salts

METHOD

Strain juice into a glass or china basin. Add all other ingredients and stir until sugar is dissolved. Bottle and seal.

To serve, pour a small amount into a tall glass. Top with chilled water or lemonade and add ice.

BUTTER

THE CROWN PRINCESS VICTORIA'S BIRTHDAY CAKE

INGREDIENTS

Walnut layer

1¼ cups walnut pieces
¼ cup icing sugar, sifted
2 egg whites

Meringue layer

2 egg whites
½ cup caster sugar
1½ cups cream, whipped
250g (8oz) fresh raspberries
Fondant or marzipan roses for decoration

METHOD

Grind walnuts in a food processor. Stir in icing sugar and mix to a paste with the unbeaten egg whites. Spread out into 2 x 20 cm (8 in) rounds on greased greaseproof paper on baking trays.

Bake in a moderate oven 10 minutes until firm to touch. Turn out onto wire racks and carefully peel off the paper. Cool.

Make meringue by beating the 2 egg whites until stiff. Add sugar gradually, beating all the time until thick. Spread out to a 20 cm (8 in) round on greased paper on a baking tray. Bake in a slow oven until dry and crisp, about 45-50 minutes. Cool and carefully remove paper.

Join the cake together on a serving plate by placing the meringue layer in the centre with whipped cream and raspberries between each layer. Completely cover with whipped cream and mould some roses from softened fondant or a marzipan roll. Colour pink with food colouring. Chill well before cutting.

SOMERSET SEED CAKE

INGREDIENTS

185g (6oz) butter
¾ cup caster sugar
2 teaspoons caraway seeds
3 eggs, separated
1 tablespoon ground almonds
2 cups self-raising flour
2 tablespoons milk
Extra caraway seeds

METHOD

Beat together butter and sugar until creamy, stir in the seeds. Beat egg whites until fairly stiff, add yolks and whisk in lightly, fold into the creamed mixture, with the almonds.

Sift the flour and fold in, with the milk. Turn into a large loaf tin, greased and lined on base with greased, greaseproof paper, top with a light sprinkling of caraway seeds. Bake in a moderate oven about 1 hour, or until done when tested. Leave in tin for 10 minutes, then turn out.

EDINBURGH SHORTBREAD

INGREDIENTS

250g (8oz) butter
½ cup caster sugar
2¼ cups plain flour
½ cup rice flour

METHOD

Cream butter and sugar. Gradually add flour and work with hands into a smooth creamy ball.

Press out on baking paper lined oven trays to form 2 x 20 cm (8 in) rounds, 1 cm (½in) thick. Pinch a frill around the edge and mark lightly into 8 wedges. Pierce all over with a fork.

Bake in a moderately slow oven 20 minutes until a pale straw colour. Cool slightly then cut through the marked lines.

PRESTON GINGERBREAD

INGREDIENTS

2 cups plain flour
¼ teaspoon nutmeg
2 teaspoons ground ginger
⅓ cup brown sugar
125g (4oz) butter
⅓ cup golden syrup
⅓ cup treacle
1 teaspoon bicarbonate of soda
1¼ cups warm milk
1 egg, lightly beaten
Slivered blanched almonds

METHOD

Sift together flour and spices, stir in the sugar. Put butter, syrup and treacle into a saucepan and gently heat until butter has melted. Stir bicarbonate of soda into the warm milk.

Add butter mixture and milk to dry ingredients, with the egg, stir in to combine well. Pour into a 28 x 18 cm (11 x 7 in) lamington tin, greased and lined on base with baking paper.

Sprinkle almonds over and bake in a moderately slow oven about 1 hour.

Following pages: Bush damper, recipe page 100 Bush Damper, was a rough bush bread of flour and water without leavening, baked on the bush campfire coals. It was part of the original staple diet of the Australian settlers. They sometimes ate it with a slab of fried dried meat, sometimes spread with; golden syrup, "bullocky's joy", always with billy tea and maybe a swig of rum.

BUSH DAMPER

INGREDIENTS

3 cups self-raising flour
2 teaspoons salt
3 tablespoons butter
½ cup milk
½ cup water

METHOD

Sift flour and salt into a bowl, rub in butter until mixture resembles fine crumbs.

Make a well in the centre, add the combined milk and water, mix lightly with a knife until dough leaves sides of bowl.

Gently knead on a lightly floured surface and then knead into a round, put on a greased oven tray. Pat into a round 15-16 cm (6-6½ in) diameter.

Bake in a hot oven for 10 minutes, or until golden brown. Reduce heat to moderate and bake another 20 minutes. Eat the day it is made. For variation, add ¾ cup grated Cheddar cheese.

POTATO SCONES

Makes 8

INGREDIENTS

250g (8oz) dry mashed potato
1 tablespoon butter
Pinch salt and pepper
¼ - ½ cup plain flour

METHOD

Place mashed potato into a basin and mix in butter, salt and pepper. Add flour gradually, adding just enough to mix into a soft, dry consistency.

Knead on a lightly floured board. Roll out thinly and cut into 8 squares or rounds.

Pierce well all over with a fork.

Cook on a greased hot griddle or frying pan 2-3 minutes. Turn when brown and cook on other side. May be served hot or cold. May be spread with butter and are delicious served with bacon.

Desiderious Orban
Morning 1959
Pastel on paper 56 x 76cm
Bathurst Regional Art Gallery

APPLE STRAWBERRY TART

Serves 6

INGREDIENTS

2 cups plain flour
155g (5oz) butter
2 tablespoons sugar
2 tablespoons cold water
3-4 cooking apples
½ cup strawberry conserve
1 egg, beaten, for glaze

METHOD

Place flour in a basin and rub in butter with fingertips. Stir in sugar.

Add water and mix into a dough. Chill.

Roll out two-thirds of the pastry and line a 23 cm (9 in) pie plate. Peel, core and slice apples into pastry case. Spread strawberry conserve over the top. Roll remaining pastry and cut into strips. Brush with egg and place in a lattice design over top and place another strip around the edge. Brush pastry again with beaten egg.

Bake in a hot oven 30 minutes until browned and cooked. Serve warm with whipped cream or ice-cream.

JAM PASTRIES

Makes about 30

INGREDIENTS

90g (3oz) butter
2 tablespoons sugar
1 teaspoon grated lemon rind
1 egg
1¾ cups plain flour
Thick raspberry jam
1 egg, beaten, for glaze
Coarse sugar

METHOD

Beat butter, sugar and lemon rind together until creamy. Beat in egg. Add flour and work into a dough. Chill thoroughly until firm enough for easy handling.

Roll out on a lightly floured surface and cut with a fluted cutter, about 8 cm (3 in). Place on greased baking trays, place a small amount of jam in the centre and fold in halves.

Brush tops with beaten egg and sprinkle with sugar. Bake in a moderate oven until cooked and lightly brown, about 15 minutes. Cool.

Opposite page: Apple Strawberry Tart

OAT WAFERS

Makes about 24

INGREDIENTS

- 1¼ cups rolled oats
- 90g (3oz) butter, melted
- 1 egg
- ¾ cup sugar
- 2 tablespoons self-raising flour

METHOD

Place oats in a bowl, pour over melted butter and allow to stand 10 minutes to soften oats slightly. Mix in egg, sugar and flour.

Place small portions well apart onto greased baking trays to allow room for spreading. Flatten out with the back of a spoon. Bake in a moderate oven 10 minutes until cooked and brown.

Allow to cool for a few minutes before removing carefully with a spatula. These delicious biscuits become crisp when cool and are worth the careful handling when removing from oven trays.

COFFEE BUTTER CAKE

INGREDIENTS

- 1¼ cups self-raising flour
- ¾ cup lightly filled brown sugar
- 2 teaspoons instant coffee
- 90g (3oz) butter, melted
- 2 eggs
- 3 tablespoons cream
- 1 x 100g block chocolate
- Blanched almonds

METHOD

Place flour, sugar and instant coffee in a bowl. Stir in melted butter, eggs and cream and beat until smooth.

Pour into a greased 5-cup loaf tin and bake in a moderate oven 35-40 minutes until cooked. Cool.

Melt chocolate gently, spread over top of cake and decorate with almonds.

Opposite page: Clockwise from right: Coffee Butter Cake, recipe page 104, Jam Pasrties, recipe page 108, and Pat Wafers, recipe above.

Margaret Preston
1875-1963
Still Life 1926
Oil on canvas 50.8 x 56cm
Bequest of Adrian Feint 1972
Art Gallery of New South Wales

WELSH RAREBIT

Serves 4

INGREDIENTS

60g (2oz) butter
1 teaspoon prepared English mustard
½ teaspoon salt
Freshly ground pepper
1 egg yolk, beaten
1 teaspoon Worcestershire sauce
125g (4oz) tasty cheese, grated
3 tablespoons beer (flat beer will do)
4 slices hot, buttered toast

METHOD

Melt the butter in a saucepan over low heat, and stir in mustard, salt and pepper to taste. Stir in egg yolk, sauce and cheese. Continue stirring until cheese melts, then stir in beer and heat through.

(Do not allow to boil.)

Taste for seasoning, and serve at once over hot buttered toast. For lunch, you might like to add pickled onions and a green salad.

NOTE: If you wish, the rarebit can be browned quickly under a hot grill after it is spread on toast.

WELSH SPECKLED BREAD (BARA BRITH)

Makes 2 loaves

INGREDIENTS

90g (3oz) butter
4 cups plain flour
½ cup brown sugar
1 cup sultanas
1 cup currants
½ cup raisins
⅓ cup chopped mixed peel
¼ teaspoon salt
½ teaspoon mixed spice
1 cup milk
1 x 7g sachet dry yeast or 15g (½ oz) compressed yeast
1 egg, beaten

METHOD

Rub butter into flour with fingertips. Stir in sugar, fruits, peel, salt and spice and make a well in the centre.

Heat milk to lukewarm and pour a little into yeast and stir until melted. Add egg yeast and remaining milk to basin and mix into a soft dough. Place in a greased bowl, cover with plastic wrap and leave in a warm place until doubled in volume, about 1 hour.

Knead thoroughly on a lightly floured surface and divide in half. Place in 2 greased 6-cup loaf tins, cover with plastic wrap and allow to stand in a warm place 30-40 minutes. Bake in a moderately hot oven 30 minutes, reduce heat to moderately slow, cover tops lightly with foil if browning too much and bake another 15-20 minutes, until cooked. This delicious Welsh teabread is served thinly sliced with butter.

Following pages: Welsh Rarebit and Welsh Speckled Bread (Bara Brith), recipes above.

Colman's
EXHIBITION
MUSTARD

IRISH SODA BREAD

Serves 4

INGREDIENTS

1 tablespoon butter
1 cup self raising flour
2 cups plain flour
1 teaspoon salt
1 teaspoon bicarbonate of soda
1 cup cooked, sieved potato
1 egg
1¼ cups buttermilk

METHOD

Rub butter into sifted dry ingredients. Mix in potato. Mix in egg beaten with half the buttermilk and gradually stir in enough remaining buttermilk to form a soft dough.

Place in a greased 20 cm (8 in) sandwich cake tin, cut a cross in the top with a sharp knife and bake in a moderately hot oven 35 minutes until cooked.

For a soft crust, brush while hot with melted butter.

WINDSOR CAKE

Serves 10-12

INGREDIENTS

250g (8oz) butter
1½ cups sugar
4 eggs
1 cup milk
4 cups self raising flour

METHOD

Beat butter and sugar until soft and creamy. Beat in eggs one at a time.

Add milk and sifted flour and beat until smooth.

Place in a greased deep 20 cm (8 in) cake tin and bake in a moderate oven until cooked, about 1¼ hours. Keeps well.

CHEESE DAMPER

INGREDIENTS

2 cups self-raising flour
½ teaspoon of salt
1 cup of milk
1½ tablespoons softened margarine
¾ cup grated Cheddar cheese

METHOD

Sift the flour and salt together. Add the milk, butter, and cheese. Beat for 1 to 2 minutes with a wooden spoon. Pour into a greased and floured 18-centimetre (7- inch) sandwich tin and bake in a hot oven for 25-30 minutes. Serve sliced with butter.

ECCLES CAKES
Makes 8

INGREDIENTS
125g (4oz) butter
2 cups plain flour
3-4 tablespoons cold water
1½ cups currants
½ cup finely chopped mixed peel
¼ cup sugar
½ teaspoon nutmeg
2 tablespoons butter
1 egg white, beaten lightly
Caster sugar

METHOD
Rub the 125 g (4 oz) butter into flour and add enough cold water to mix into a firm dough. Chill. Place currants, mixed peel, sugar, nutmeg and the 2 tablespoons butter into a saucepan and stir over a low heat until butter melts. Pour into a basin and allow to cool.

Roll out pastry and cut into 8 rounds, using a saucer. Divide fruit mixture between the circles, gather up edges and pinch together. Turn over, roll lightly and brush with the egg white. Sprinkle with caster sugar and make 3 small slits in the top.

Place on greased baking trays and bake in a hot oven 15-20 minutes until lightly browned.

APPLE SPONGE
Serves 4-5

INGREDIENTS
1 cup self raising flour
Pinch salt
½ cup caster sugar
1 egg
90g (3oz) butter, melted
4 cooking apples, peeled and sliced

METHOD
Place flour, salt and sugar in a basin. Beat in egg and melted butter.

Place apples in a greased shallow 5-cup ovenproof dish.

Spoon cake mixture over apples and bake in a moderate oven 45-50 minutes until cooked.

Serve warm with whipped cream or custard.

CHEESE FLAN

Serves 6-8

INGREDIENTS

- 125g (4oz) butter
- 2 cups plain flour
- 3 tablespoons cold water
- 125g (4oz) tasty cheese, cut into small cubes
- 125g (4oz) Swiss cheese, cut into small cubes
- 1 small onion, grated
- 4 eggs
- ¾ cup cream
- ½ cup sour cream
- 2 tablespoons grated Parmesan cheese
- ½ teaspoon paprika
- Salt and pepper

METHOD

Make pastry by rubbing butter into the flour and mix into a dough with the water. Chill 1 hour. Press evenly over base and sides of a fluted 28 cm (11 in) flan tin with removable base.

Pierce well with a fork and bake in a hot oven 10 minutes.

Combine tasty cheese, Swiss cheese and grated onion. Place evenly over base of pastry.

Beat eggs, cream, sour cream and Parmesan cheese together. Season with paprika, salt and pepper to taste and pour into pastry case.

Return to oven and bake a further 30-35 minutes until cooked. If topping is browning too much, cover lightly with a piece of foil. Serve freshly made with salad.

ORANGE BREAD

INGREDIENTS

- 1 tablespoon finely grated orange rind
- 60g (2oz) margarine
- ½ cup sugar
- 1 egg
- 1½ cups self-raising flour
- ½ cup milk
- chopped mixed peel
- extra sugar

METHOD

Work the orange rind into the margarine then gradually beat in the sugar. Add the egg and beat in well. Sift the flour and fold alternately with the milk. Turn into a greased 20 x 10 centimetre (8 x 4 in) loaf tin. Smooth the surface and sprinkle lightly with the chopped mixed peel and extra sugar. Bake in a moderately hot oven for about 35 minutes, or until done when tested.

Opposite page: Cheese Flan, recipe above.

E. Phillips Fox

The Second Hundred Years

E. Phillips Fox
1865–1915
The Arbour 1910
Oil on canvas 190.5 x 230.7cm
Felton Bequest 1916
National Gallery of Victoria, Melbourne

Margaret Preston
1875–1963
Implement Blue 1927
Oil on canvas on paperboard
42.5 x 43cm
Gift of the artist 1960
Art Gallery of New South Wales

The Second Hundred Years

Lamingtons, as all Australians know are simply squares of plain cake dipped in melted chocolate and sugar and coated in desiccated coconut. They are supposed to have been named after Baron Lamington, governor of Queensland from 1895 to 1901.

Peach Melba was created in 1894 by Escoffier in honour of the Australian singer Dame Nellie Melba. It consists of a fresh peach poached in vanilla-flavoured sugar syrup, peeled, set on a layer of icecream, coated with fresh raspberry purée and served in an individual or crystal dish.

These two confections, and damper, were probably the only culinary inventions which Australia could call her own at the turn-of the-century. Between Federation in 1901 and the end of the Great War in 1918, our food habits didn't change much, apart from the necessary wartime tightening of belts. Patriotic cookery books of the time popularised a few new recipes such as Anzac Biscuits and Soldier's Christmas Cake, which anxious wives and mothers lovingly baked and packed in food parcels to send to the trenches.

The average Australian takes no aesthetic pleasure in food scoffed the Melbourne playwright, Louis Esson in 1918. However, at the end of the 19th century, speculation, building and land development, had spawned visions of wealth and power which spilled over into the 20th. Prosperity had produced a fashion for grand balls, receptions and large public banquets to honour special events or people, such as the Grand Federation Dinner in January, 1901. These were outstanding affairs, not for average Australians, but for the elite, the officials and politicians. Menus were elaborate but uninspired, with a profusion of Anglo-French dishes, and an embarrassment of wines, especially French champagne. Here is a menu for one consular dinner celebrating Queen Victoria's birthday:

Salad Russe
Cressy Soup
Clear Soup
Whiting Timbale
Schnapper grilled á la Tartare

Entrée
Vol-au-vent of Spring Chicken
Sweetbread with Tomato Sauce
Roast Turkey

Removes
Grilled Ham
Fillet of Lamb with Olives
Charlotte of Apples
Pineapple Cream
Nessebrode Pudding
Findon Haddock on Toast
Cheese Fritter

Champagne luncheons featuring cold fowl and ham, as well as wines and beer, were a fashionable pursuit among the new moneyed society in this age of opulence. They were customary at public land sales, big auctions and race meetings. Picnics on a grand scale

were another. In 1868 when Prince Edward, Duke of Edinburgh, was visiting Australia, at a picnic in his honour in Sydney, guests ate fresh oysters, bread and butter and stout in the morning, lobster, chicken and champagne in the afternoon.

The boom in restaurants which had begun with the Gold Rush and popularised mixed grills and carpetbag steak, continued into the 20th century as the population increased. The first free settlers had begun arriving in the 1820s, full of vitality and optimism. They continued to pour in until the first government immigration schemes began and the country grew from a colony to a nation. The divisions of the classes were still strictly defined, but these working class people were the harbingers of the rising middle class which would eventually dominate the structure of our emerging society and its cuisine.

Blancmanges and trifles were wrapped in wet cloths and carried in their moulds by buggy to celebrations where the community shared their food.

Dining at home depended on wealth and status. In the towns, for the very rich and well-to-do, it was elaborate and formal. For the working class it was simple, revolving around roast meat with gravy, baked potatoes and vegetables, and a pudding, for midday dinner every Sunday. On Monday, the meat was eaten cold, perhaps with shredded lettuce salad and homemade boiled mayonnaise. Thus, for the poor, dining was a monotonous, usually inadequate affair.

When a young married newspaperman, Joseph Elliott, wrote home to his mother in England describing his family life in their Adelaide cottage in the 1860s, he was simply reinforcing an established way of life perpetuated by ordinary people: *Well, after Church (on Sunday), we dine in our sitting room, and come when you will, you will always find the same dinner! We consume 52 legs of mutton a year! Baked in the oven and also a few baked potatoes. After that we have English jam tarts or something of the sort but generally the tarts are preferred, at all events six or seven months out of the twelve. After that we generally have a few apples or something of the sort. Monday. I get to town between 8 and 9, taking some lunch with me for 1 o'clock, leave town at about 5 and dine on cold mutton and warm potatoes with mint sauce, of which I am very fond. Tuesday. We generally dine on either mutton or beef; beef or mutton—not much change here.*[5]

In Sydney and Melbourne in the 20s, life was busy and colourful, with thriving markets and a multitude of busy pubs. The clip clop of the baker's carthorse or the rattle of milk bottles in the street at dawn were familiar sounds. Chinese vegetable men, rabbit and fish sellers and street market stalls were familiar sights as they had been since the 1850s when food vendors with old cries, tempted passers-by to pig's trotters, saveloys and bottled oysters. In Sydney, Charlie the Pieman carried his hot chicken, meat and cherry pies about in a basket. Little meat pies eaten hot with tomato sauce eventually became an Australian institution. With the linking of the railway lines and more opportunities for travel, they were nicknamed 'railway pies', and in some parts of the country eaten in bowls of thick pea soup and called 'floaters'.

Meanwhile, in the bush, life went on as it had since the opening up of rich pasture lands on the Bathurst Plains a hundred years before. It was a struggle for the 'cockatoo farmers' or 'cockles' as the smallholders were called, but a life of comparative ease for the 'silver tails', the bush aristocracy with their sprawling homesteads and enormous properties. They had mahogany furniture, polished cedar floors, fine china, silver and glass and kept house servants. These landowning families played a paternal role to their employees, the station hands, stockmen and shearers who ate meat three times a day and got drunk on Saturdays.

But in the wattle and daub huts of the poorest settlers, life was hard. They lived off the land, and women worked as hard as the men. They preserved their food by salting, drying, boiling in sugar syrup or fermenting. They cooked on open fires or camp ovens, made bread, butter, cheese and soap; dug potatoes, grew vegetables, dried their fruit, cured bacon and carried

[5] *Our Home in Australia. A Description of Cottage Life in 1860 by Joseph Elliott. The Flannel Flower Press. Sydney, 1984.*

water. Their store rooms were filled with their own jams, pickles, chutneys, preserves, cordials, ginger beer and cough mixture. Despite loneliness, heat, dust, blowflies, bushfires and drought, the strongest survived.

For recreation there were bush dances, travelling circuses, church suppers, country shows and race meetings, weddings, christenings and funerals. In this environment women cultivated their skills in baking and struggled to produce decent family meals. There were no ice chests or refrigeration, only Coolgardie safes and ingenuity. Jellies were made with isinglass. Blancmanges and trifles were wrapped in wet cloths and carried in their moulds by buggy to celebrations where the community shared their food.

From no ice to ice boxes to refrigerators; from wood stoves to gas to electricity; with advances in food technology and transport, and the introduction of canning and freezing, the old-fashioned Australian diet began to stir itself into the 20th century.

In many ways, 1929 was significant. It was the first year of the Depression which lasted into the mid-30s. Unemployment, dole queues, austerity meals and soup kitchens took much of the fun out of life, which the cinema replaced with celluloid dreams of romance and escape. 'Swaggies', itinerant unemployed men, wandered the country with their swags on their backs and only their dogs for company, looking for work outside the cities.

This was the year that Chef Herbert Sachse of the Hotel Esplanade in Perth, invented the pavlova, in honour of Anna Pavlova. It was a symphony of meringue, cream and passionfruit to celebrate the great Russian ballerina's visit.

In 1929 the first of the stream of persecuted Jews fleeing from the regimes of Hitler and Mussolini began to flow in. We called them 'refugees'. Many of them set up Polish-Austrian-German style delicatessens, butcher shops, bakeries and patisseries, stimulating our 'meat and potatoes' appetites with flavour sensations from their old traditional backgrounds.

When the Second World War broke out in 1939, the American troops who came to the Pacific intrigued us even more with their hamburgers, hot dogs, club sandwiches, milk shakes, Coca Cola, chicken Maryland, Boston baked beans and barbecues.

By 1947, with the fall of Singapore, an influx of Dutch civilians escaping from the Japanese added their Dutch-Indonesian dishes to our repertoire. Nasi goreng and rijsttafel joined the curries and other exotic dishes we had inherited earlier from the British Raj, such as kedgeree, and mulligatawny.

Post-war, immigration from Europe and the Mediterranean countries revolutionised our food habits forever. Italians, Greeks and new arrivals from all over the world introduced us to garlic, herbs, pasta, tomato paste, patés and terrines, and all the other delights of their culinary heritages.

Mrs Beeton was the food guru of the 19th century, and Elizabeth David was the leader of the new wave of cookery we fell in love with after the war. *Mediterranean Food*, her first cookery book, was published in England in 1950, and followed by others. They made a great impression on Australian women, and coincided with their burgeoning interest in food from other lands, as well as setting off the phenomenal 20th century avalanche of cookbooks, many of the best by Australians.

We have grown used to food cults and fads. We have learned that nutrition, good health, fitness and sensible eating can influence our life spans. Vegetarian cookery, health foods, macrobiotics, slimming diets, and *nouvelle cuisine* have contributed to our improved eating habits and food presentation. Proliferating restaurants, supermarkets, speciality food shops, caterers, takeaways, microwave ovens, electrical gadgets and convenience foods have simplified our lives. The impact of the working woman, with less time to spend on cooking, is still an unknown quantity. Food gurus on radio, television and in magazines and newspapers, colour food photography, professional *bon vivants* and consultants, cooking schools, and food advertising campaigns have intensified our interest in gastronomy.

Today our population has been stimulated by a huge proportion of people from other countries. We share a

utmeg, Sour cream, Parsley, chopped, Croûtons, method; Peel, remove
nd salt. Pour in just enough water to cover and cook gently, with the li
food processor with the milks (or push through a sieve and then stir i
over and simmer for 5-7 minutes. Serve with a swirl of sour cream ar
eparately. 750g (1/2 lb) pumpkin, 1 medium onion, chopped, 1 teaspoo
eam, Parsley, chopped, Croûtons, method; Peel, remove seeds from pun
just enough water to cover and cook gently, with the lid on, until the p
ith the milks (or push through a sieve and then stir in the milk). Return
r 5-7 minutes. Serve with a swirl of sour cream and a sprinkling of pa
move seeds from pumpkin, and cut into pieces. Put into a saucepan wi

Soups

s from pumpkin, and cut into pieces. Put into a saucepan with the onio
, until the pumpkin is tender. Purée the contents of the pan in a blend
e milk). Return the purée to the saucepan, adding the sugar and nutme
sprinkling of parsley on each bowl and serve a bowl of crisp croûton
t, Water, 2 cups milk, 2 teaspoons sugar, Pinch of grated nutmeg, So
n, and cut into pieces. Put into a saucepan with the onion and salt. Po
kin is tender. Purée the contents of the pan in a blender or food process
purée to the saucepan, adding the sugar and nutmeg. Cover and simm
y on each bowl Sour cream, Parsley, chopped, Croûtons, method; Pe
he onion and salt. Pour in just enough water

BORSCH

Serves 8

INGREDIENTS

1kg (2lb) shin of beef
8 cups water
1 onion, chopped
3 bay leaves
1 tablespoon whole allspice
2 teaspoons salt
2 tomatoes, peeled and chopped
2 potatoes, cut into thin strips
2 carrots, cut into thin strips
1 small cabbage, shredded
750g (1½lb) beetroot, cut into thin strips
2 teaspoons vinegar
Salt and freshly ground pepper
¼ cup chopped parsley
2 tablespoons snipped fresh dill

METHOD

Place beef, water, onion, bay leaves, allspice and salt into a large saucepan and bring to boil. Skim if necessary and cook with lid on for 1 hour or until tender.

While meat is cooking collect all the vegetables together. It is best to be patient and use a sharp knife to cut the vegetables (if they are grated the soup will be cloudy).

When meat is cooked remove from the pot. Cut into thick strips from the bone and place meat back into the pot. Add all the vegetables and allow to boil without the lid for about 15 minutes. If you cook with the lid on, the soup will not retain its bright attractive colour.

Stir in vinegar, salt, pepper, parsley and dill. Serve piping hot with a spoonful of whipped cream flavoured with horseradish cream and black bread.

Opposite page:
Borsch, recipe above.

CHILLED CUCUMBER YOGHURT SOUP

Serves 4

INGREDIENTS

- 1 medium-sized cucumber
- 1 teaspoon salt
- 1 large clove garlic
- 1 tablespoon wine vinegar
- 2 teaspoons finely chopped fresh dill
- 2 cups natural yoghurt
- 1 tablespoon chopped fresh mint

METHOD

Peel cucumber if necessary and slice thinly. Sprinkle with the salt. Rub a bowl with the cut garlic clove and pour in the vinegar, dill and yoghurt. Stir thoroughly.

Mix in the cucumber slices and sprinkle mint over the top.

Chill for about 5 minutes in freezer and serve.

PROVENÇALE VEGETABLE SOUP

Serves 6-8

INGREDIENTS

- 6 cups water
- 1 cup diced potato
- 1 cup diced carrot
- 1 large leek, cut into strips
- 1 cup sliced green beans
- Salt
- 1 x 310g can butter beans
- ½ cup broken pieces spaghetti
- ½ cup soft breadcrumbs
- 2 cloves garlic
- 2 tablespoons tomato paste
- 2 tablespoons fresh basil leaves
- ¼ cup grated Parmesan cheese
- 1 teaspoon curry paste
- 2 tablespoons olive oil

METHOD

Place water in a large saucepan, add potato, carrot, leek, green beans and salt to taste.

Cook for 20 minutes with lid on. Add butter beans, spaghetti and breadcrumbs and cook another 15-20 minutes until spaghetti is tender.

Pulverise garlic, tomato paste, basil, Parmesan and curry paste in a blender. Beat in olive oil a few drops at a time. If desired may be worked to a paste with a pestle and mortar.

Stir into hot soup and serve.

CHILLED AVOCADO SOUP

Serves 4

INGREDIENTS

2 large ripe avocados, peeled and stoned
3 cups strong chicken stock
2 teaspoons lemon juice
Salt and freshly ground pepper
½ cup cream
Extra cream, whipped
Watercress

METHOD

Purée avocados in a blender with chicken stock and lemon juice.

Stir in salt, pepper and cream. Chill thoroughly.

Serve in bowls, topped with a little whipped cream and chopped watercress.

GREEK CHICKEN SOUP

Serves 6-8

INGREDIENTS

1 x 1kg (2lb) chicken
6 cups water
1 carrot sliced
1 onion sliced
1 stalk celery, sliced
1 teaspoon fresh thyme
1 bay leaf
2 garlic cloves, chopped
Salt to taste
2 teaspoons whole white peppercorns
¼ cup rice
1 tablespoon vegetable oil
1 egg yolk
2 eggs
Juice 1 lemon
Snipped chives

METHOD

Place chicken, water, carrot, onion, celery, thyme, bay leaf, garlic, salt and peppercorns in a large saucepan. Bring to boil, skim if necessary and cook until chicken is tender.

Remove chicken from stock and allow to cool. Cut into small pieces.

Strain stock and chill. Remove fat from top of stock. Sauté rice in the hot oil for a few minutes, add to the chicken stock and cook 15-18 minutes until rice is cooked. Stir in chicken. Taste for seasoning and add more salt and pepper if necessary. If a more filling soup is desired, double the amount of rice.

Beat egg yolk, eggs and lemon juice together and carefully beat in to this a little of the hot soup. Add. this to the rest of the hot soup, stirring all the time. Do not allow to boil, only re-heat, otherwise the soup will curdle. Serve immediately with bread and cheese.

Sprinkle snipped chives over top.

Following pages: Clockwise from top right: Provençale Vegetable Soup, recipe page 126; Seafood Soup, recipe page 130; Greek Chicken Soup, recipe above.

CREAMY PRAWN SOUP

Serves 4

INGREDIENTS

1kg (2lb) prawns
1 onion, chopped
1 cup chopped celery (include green tops)
4 cups water
2 tablespoons butter
2 tablespoons flour
Salt and pepper
1 tablespoon tomato paste
½ cup dry white wine
½ cup cream

METHOD

Shell prawns and reserve a few for garnish. Place the remainder in a food processor and purée.

Place prawn shells, onion and celery in the water and bring to boil. Cook 20 minutes and then allow to cool. Strain.

Melt butter, add flour, salt and pepper to taste and stir 2-3 minutes over a low heat.

Add prawn liquid and stir until thickened and boiling. Stir in tomato paste and wine and cook gently 10 minutes.

Stir in puréed prawns and cream and heat through gently. Do not allow to boil because this may cause the soup to curdle. Place in warmed soup bowls and garnish with whipped cream, the reserved prawns and fine strips of lemon rind.

SEAFOOD SOUP

Serves 4-6

INGREDIENTS

1 leek
1 fennel bulb
½ cup sliced celery
8 mushrooms, sliced
1 clove garlic, crushed
3 tablespoons olive oil
4 cups fish stock
1 bay leaf
2 teaspoons lemon juice
Salt and pepper
500g (1lb) gemfish, diced
125g (4oz) scallops
4-6 scampi or king prawns, shelled
¼ cup dry white wine
½ cup whole egg mayonnaise
3 cloves garlic, crushed
Croûtons

METHOD

Wash leek and cut into strips together with the fennel bulb.

Add celery, mushrooms, garlic and cook in the hot oil for 10 minutes. Stir in fish stock, bay leaf, lemon juice, salt and pepper to taste. Simmer 5 minutes.

Add diced fish and scallops and cook gently 5 minutes. Stir in scampi or king prawns, wine and taste to see if more seasoning is needed. Re-heat gently.

Mix mayonnaise and garlic together, if too thick stir in some cream. Serve soup in bowls with croûtons and spoon on a little of the mayonnaise mixture.

Opposite page: Creamy Prawn Soup, recipe above.

Margaret Preston
1875–1963
Thea Proctor's Tea Party 1924
Oil on canvas 55.9 x 45.7cm
purchased 1942
Art Gallery of New South Wales

TUNA CHOWDER

Serves 4-6

INGREDIENTS

250g (8oz) potatoes, peeled and diced
1 tablespoon butter
2 bacon rashers, cut into small squares, with rind removed
2 medium onions, thinly sliced
1 x 375ml can evaporated milk
Salt and pepper
1 x 425g can tuna
Chopped parsley

METHOD

Cook the potatoes in 2 cups of boiling salted water for about 8 minutes; remove the pan from the heat. Melt the butter and gently fry the bacon and onions until the onions are transparent and the bacon is crisp; drain and add to the potatoes in the saucepan. Gradually stir in the evaporated milk, then season with salt and pepper. Simmer for 10 minutes. Drain and flake the tuna, add to pan, and simmer for 5-7 minutes, or until heated through.

Sprinkle with chopped parsley.

CHICKEN NOODLE SOUP

Serves 4-6

INGREDIENTS

1 cooked boiling fowl (see recipe Settler's Chicken, page 40)
250g (8oz) noodles
4 cups chicken stock (see recipe Settler's Chicken, page 40)
Salt and pepper
¼ cup chopped parsley

METHOD

Remove chicken skin and bones and cut flesh into bite-sized pieces. Cook noodles in boiling salted water until almost tender. Drain and add to hot chicken stock with chicken pieces. Taste for seasoning.

Bring slowly to boil and simmer. Serve hot.

gredients 500 g (1lb) firm-fleshed fish fillets 13/4 cups water 1 small cel
(4oz) scallops, split into halves 185 g (6oz) small mushrooms, thinly slic
:og (8oz) prawns, shelled and deveined Buttered breadcrumbs method R
eat the water with the celery, onion, parsley, bay leaf, and wine unt
emove the fish with a slotted spoon and put aside. Add the scallops to
easure and reserve 11/4 cups. Cook the mushrooms and shallots gently
aped individual ovenproof dishes, or into a shallow ovenproof dish. M
e reserved fish stock and cook, stirring until boiling. Simmer for 3-4 mi
3 minutes to reheat. Spoon into the dishes or dish. Top with buttered
edium heat until crisp). Put into a hot oven to reheat. Remove the fish

Seafood

talk 1/2 small onion 2 parsley sprigs 1 bay leaf 2/3 cup dry white wine 1
shallots, finely chopped Butter Salt and pepper 1 tablespoon plain flo
ve skin from the fish and cut the flesh into small cubes, taking out bone
oiling. Simmer for 5 minutes. Add the fish and simmer until just tend
pan and simmer for 5 minutes. Remove the scallops and strain the liqu
butter until softened. Add salt and pepper to taste. Spoon into 4-6 she
1 tablespoon butter, add the flour, and stir for a minute. Gradually a
es. Add salt and pepper, then the fish, prawns, and scallops. Simmer f
mbs (about 6 tablespoons tossed in 3 tablespoons of melted butter ov
h a slotted spoon and put aside. Add the scallops to the pan and simm

SMOKED SALMON APPETISERS

Serves 4

INGREDIENTS

4 bread slices, buttered
4 smoked salmon slices
½ cup whipped cream
1 teaspoon horseradish cream
250g (8oz) prawns, shelled

METHOD

Fry bread on both sides until crisp and brown. Place on small serving plates and cover with smoked salmon.

Mix cream and horseradish together, spoon onto salmon and top with prawns.

Garnish with a sprig of fresh dill.

CREAMED MUSSELS

Serves 6 entrées

INGREDIENTS

36 fresh mussels
Water to cover
60g (2oz) butter
2 tablespoons plain flour
1½ cups cooking liquid from mussels
1 clove garlic, crushed
⅓ cup dry white wine
2 egg yolks
2 tablespoons lemon juice
⅓ cup cream
Salt and freshly ground pepper
Finely chopped parsley to garnish

METHOD

Wash mussels in cold, running water and scrub with a stiff brush until clean. Discard any that are not tightly closed. Place in a wide saucepan, cover with boiling water, and boil rapidly for 5 minutes, or until they open. Discard any that do not open.

Remove mussels from their shells, reserving the best shells for serving the mussels.

Strain the cooking liquid and save 1⅓ cups.

Melt the butter, stir in flour over low heat, and cook for 1 minute. Remove from heat and stir in the warm cooking liquid and the garlic. Bring to the boil and simmer for 5 minutes. Whisk wine, egg yolks, lemon juice and cream together and stir into pan. Continue stirring ntil sauce thickens, and season to taste with salt and pepper. Return mussels to the pan and gently reheat. Spoon into shells and sprinkle with chopped parsley.

Opposite page: Smoked Salmon Appetisers, recipe above.

Eric Wilson 1911–1946
Abstract - The Kitchen
Stove, 1943
Oil, paper on plywood 145.5 x 79.7cm
Gift of the New South Wales
Travelling Art Scholarship
Committee 1946
Art Gallery of New South Wales

SALMON MOUSSE

Serves 4-6

INGREDIENTS

6 teaspoons gelatine
¼ cup hot water
½ cup evaporated milk or cream
¼ cup vinegar or lemon juice
½ teaspoon dry mustard
½ teaspoon salt
¼ teaspoon freshly ground black pepper
Pinch of nutmeg
1 x 220 g can salmon
1 medium cucumber, peeled, grated, and thoroughly drained
1 teaspoon caster sugar
¼ cup hot water
½ cup tomato juice
2 medium celery stalks, finely chopped
4 shallots, finely chopped

Sour cream dressing

⅔ cup sour cream
1 teaspoon horseradish relish
1 teaspoon snipped chives 1 teaspoon chopped parsley
Pinch of salt
Pinch of cayenne pepper
1 teaspoon vinegar

METHOD

Sprinkle 3 teaspoons of the gelatine into ¼ cup of the hot water, stirring until thoroughly dissolved. Leave to cool slightly. Whisk the evaporated milk with the vinegar or lemon juice, the mustard, salt, black pepper, and nutmeg. Stir in the cooled gelatine. Add the flaked undrained salmon and the cucumber, mixing well. Pour into a mould that has been rinsed with cold water. Put in the refrigerator and leave until set. Meanwhile, dissolve the remaining 3 teaspoons of gelatine and the caster sugar in the remaining ¼ cup of hot water.

Stir in the tomato juice, celery, and shallots. Carefully spoon over the set layer of salmon.

Chill for at least 4 hours. Carefully turn out on to a platter and serve with the dressing.

Sour cream dressing: Mix all ingredients together.

COROMANDEL PRAWNS

Serves 4-5

INGREDIENTS

60g (2oz) butter
2 teaspoons curry powder
4 shallots, sliced
1 clove garlic, crushed
1 capsicum, sliced
¾ cup evaporated milk
1 tablespoon tomato paste
2 teaspoons soy sauce
½ cup sour cream
1 tablespoon dry sherry
750g (1½lb) prawns, shelled
1 x 250g packet frozen spinach, thawed

METHOD

Melt butter, add curry powder, shallots, garlic and capsicum and cook for a few minutes until softened. Stir in evaporated milk, tomato paste and soy sauce and cook gently 3-4 minutes.

Add sour cream, sherry and prawns and stir until evenly mixed and hot. Do not cook any longer at this stage.

Press water out of spinach and cook until tender. Drain, place on serving dish and top with the curried prawns. Serve with rice or lots of crusty bread.

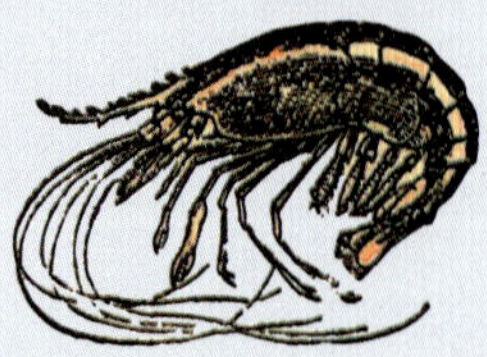

SALMON BAKE

Serves 4

INGREDIENTS

8 boiled new potatoes
1 leek, sliced
1 x 185g can salmon, drained
3 eggs
1½ cups milk
1 tablespoon chopped fresh dill
Salt and pepper

METHOD

Slice potatoes and place alternate layers in a greased ovenproof dish together with leek and salmon.

Beat eggs and milk together. Stir in dill, salt and pepper to taste. Pour into ovenproof dish.

Bake in a moderately hot oven until set, about 30 minutes. Delicious with carrot salad.

Right: Coromandel Prawns, recipe above

ESTD.
1876
MANGO CHUTNEY
& SONS PRIVATE LTD.

CRAB TARTLETS

Makes aout 24

INGREDIENTS

2 cups plain flour
½ teaspoon baking powder
Pinch of salt
155g (5oz) butter, chopped
1 egg yolk, mixed with 3 tablespoons cold water
1 x 155 g can crab, drained and flaked
60g (2oz) Swiss cheese, shredded
½ cup sour cream
1 tablespoon mayonnaise
1 egg, beaten
⅓ cup cream
Salt
Pinch of cayenne pepper
Pinch of nutmeg
1 tablespoon finely chopped parsley

METHOD

Sift the flour, baking powder, and salt into a mixing bowl. Add the butter and rub until the mixture resembles breadcrumbs. Add the egg yolk and water and mix to a firm dough (add a little more water if too dry). Wrap in plastic and chill in the refrigerator for about 30 minutes. Roll out the dough to a thickness of 5 mm (¼ in) and cut into rounds to fit into patty tins. Line the tins with the pastry and prick the bases very lightly.

Mix the crab with the cheese and spoon into the pastry cases. Mix the sour cream with mayonnaise, egg, cream, salt to taste, cayenne pepper, nutmeg, and parsley. Spoon over the crab mixture. Bake in a moderately hot oven until the pastry has browned and the filling has set. Carefully remove from the patty tins and serve warm or cold.

OYSTERS KILPATRICK

Serves 4

INGREDIENTS

½ cup tomato sauce
1 tablespoon Worcestershire sauce
Juice of 1 medium lemon
24 oysters on the shell
Salt and pepper
48 small bacon strips

METHOD

Combine sauces and lemon juice. Pour over each oyster. Cover with two bacon strips. Grill quickly until the bacon is crisp.

TROUT ALMONDINE

Serves 4

INGREDIENTS

4 medium trout
Salt
Plain flour
Salt and pepper
125g (4oz) butter
2 teaspoons lemon juice
Freshly ground pepper
⅓ cup blanched almonds, toasted and split into halves
Lemon wedges

METHOD

Trim the fins of each trout close to the body, leaving the head and tails intact.

Sprinkle the inside of the trout with salt and toss in the flour seasoned with salt and pepper.

Melt half the butter in a frying pan. Add the fish and cook until browned underneath.

Turn and brown the other side.

Carefully lift the fish on to a heated serving platter and keep warm. Add the rest of the butter to the pan with the lemon juice, pepper, and almonds. Cook, stirring, for 2-3 minutes. Pour over the fish and serve at once with the lemon wedges. Serve with salads.

BAKED FISH WITH HERB STUFFING

Serves 4-6

INGREDIENTS

1 large snapper or other whole fish
125g (4oz) butter
2 cups bread cubes
4 rashers of bacon, chopped
1 small clove garlic, crushed
1 stick of celery, sliced
3 shallots, finely chopped
1 tablespoon chopped fresh thyme, or 1 teaspoon dried
Salt and freshly ground pepper
A little melted butter
Sliced limes or lemons to garnish

METHOD

Wipe cavity of fish and place fish on an oiled baking dish. Heat butter in a large pan, add bread cubes and fry until crisp and golden. Remove from pan and set aside to cool.

Place bacon in the same pan, and fry until the fat runs. Add garlic, celery and shallots and cook until soft, about 5 minutes. Combine with bread cubes, herbs, salt and pepper.

Spoon filling into the fish and brush fish with melted butter. Bake in a preheated moderate oven for about ¾ hour, or until flesh is white and opaque and flakes easily when tested with a fork. To serve, cut fish into slices and serve each with a spoonful of herbed bread stuffing. Garnish with lime or lemon slices.

Following pages: Pan Fried Trout, freshly caught in the Snowy Mountains, or some bubbling high-country stream, makes a heavenly outdoor meal. In our photograph, it is served with new potato salad and baby beetroot tossed in mayonnaise and herbs. Trout Almondine, recipe above, is a more sophisticated presentation of this delectable fish.

CLASSIFIEDS
PHONE: 652-2222
BIRTHDAY GREETINGS
21ST BIRTHDAY
ROSSLYN SCHOTT
Jets shadow US plane
WASHINGTON

VIN D'ALSACE
ALSACE
PRODUCT OF

SKEWERED PRAWNS WITH CHILLI MAYONNAISE AND AVOCADO CREAM

Serves 2

INGREDIENTS

18 medium-sized green king prawns
4 tablespoons vegetable oil
1 tablespoon lemon juice
½ teaspoon dried tarragon
2 zucchini, sliced

Chilli Mayonnaise

¼ cup whole egg mayonnaise
1 tablespoon tomato sauce
¼ teaspoon ground chillies

Avocado cream

1 ripe avocado
1 clove garlic, crushed
2 tablespoons whole egg mayonnaise

METHOD

Shell prawns and place in a bowl. Mix together oil, lemon juice and tarragon.

Pour over prawns and mix well. Thread onto 2 skewers with alternate slices of zucchini.

Brush with the marinade.

Grill, turning often and brushing with remaining marinade until prawns turn pink.

Serve with saffron rice, Chilli Mayonnaise and Avocado Cream.

Chilli mayonnaise: Mix all ingredients together.

Avocado cream: Mash avocado and stir in garlic and mayonnaise.

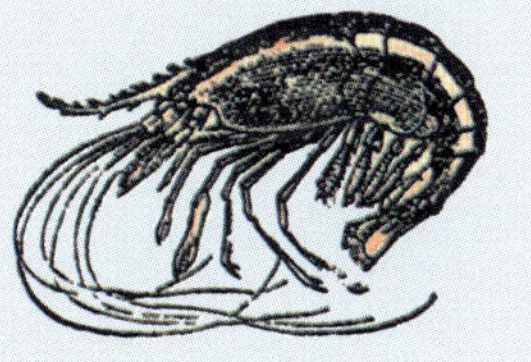

Opposite page: Skewered Prawns with Chilli Mayonnaise and Avocado Cream, recipe above.

BARBECUED FISH IN FOIL

Serves 4

INGREDIENTS

1kg (2lb) snapper, bream, or jewfish
Garlic salt
Lemon pepper
1 tablespoon butter
Salt
2 tablespoons chopped shallots
¾ cup chopped mushrooms
2 tablespoons chopped parsley
1 medium lemon

METHOD

Make three diagonal incisions about 2.5cm (1in) apart on each side of the fish, in the thickest part. Sprinkle inside of fish with garlic salt and lemon pepper. Brush both sides of the fish with melted butter and sprinkle with salt and lemon pepper.

Melt butter and gently fry the shallots and chopped mushrooms until softened. Stir in parsley. Spoon mixture into cavity of fish and add two or three slices of lemon.

Secure opening with small skewers.

Lightly butter a piece of heavy foil large enough to enclose the fish. Put fish in centre and squeeze over juice from rest of lemon. Bring edges of foil up and fold loosely over fish enclosing it completely. Barbecue until tender when tested with a fork.

Still Life with Fish
Arthur Murch
Oil on board 33.5 x 44cm
Bathurst Regional Art Gallery

x 3kg (6lb) goose 21/2 tablespoons plain flour 3 tablespoons brandy 11/2
blespoons butter 1large onion, chopped 2 Granny Smith apples, peeled,
day-old bread, toasted in the oven 2 teaspoons finely grated lemon
aspoon dried thyme Salt and pepper to taste method Make the stuffi
ith damp paper towels. Remove the oil sac from the parsonis nose, using
secure with poultry pins. Truss the bird, then wipe over with paper to
a lightly oiled baking dish. Put the dish over high heat and sear the bi
r 15 minutes. Baste, cover with foil, and reduce the temperature to mod
the cooking time. Transfer to a heated serving platter, remove the
blespoons of juice from the pan, add the remaining tablespoon of flour,

Poultry

s stock made from neck and giblets of goose, or chicken stock Stuffing
ed, and diced 1 1/2 cups chopped stoned soft prunes 31/2 cups small cub
1/4 cup chopped parsley 1 teaspoon snipped fresh thyme leaves or 1
Remove excess fat from the inside of the goose. Wipe inside and outsic
hen scissors. Fill the cavity loosely with the stuffing. Sew up the openir
s to dry thoroughly. Sprinkle 1 1/2å tablespoons of the flour over and p
Varm the brandy, set alight, and pour over the goose. Roast in a hot ove
e. Roast for 21/2 hours, removing the foil about 30 minutes before the er
ssing string, and keep warm while you make the gravy. Pour all but
d stir over medium heat until browned, scraping up the pan juices. Slow

CHICKEN MARYLAND

Serves 4-8

INGREDIENTS

½ cup flour
1 teaspoon salt
½ teaspoon ground pepper
1 egg
2 tablespoons water
1 x 1.25-1.5kg (2½-3lb) chicken, cut in 8 pieces
2 cups fine dry breadcrumbs
Oil for frying
Tomatoes
Pineapple slices
Bananas
Potatoes
Sweetcorn
Green peas
Watercress or parsley

METHOD

Mix the flour with the salt and pepper. Lightly beat the egg in a shallow bowl with the water. Coat the chicken pieces with the seasoned flour, dip in egg mixture and roll in breadcrumbs.

Heat oil in a heavy frying pan and fry the chicken gently about 20 minutes, turning often with tongs, until crisp and brown and cooked. Drain on paper towels and keep warm. Serve chicken portions on individual plates with traditional American Chicken Maryland accompaniments such as grilled tomato halves, pineapple slices and bananas, little sweetcorn patties or balls, potato balls or chips, green peas and watercress or parsley garnish.

A Second World War newcomer from the United States and a surprise to palates not familiar with the sweet taste of fruit with chicken, Chicken Maryland was often served in restaurants with coleslaw, and followed by a Banana Split for dessert. Chicken Maryland, recipe page 152, with corn fritters, fried banana, pineapple, stuffed tomato, potato puffs and peas.

ITALIAN LEMON CHICKEN

Serves 4-5

INGREDIENTS

1.5kg (3lb) small chicken pieces
Salt and pepper
½ teaspoon dried rosemary
¼ cup vegetable oil
1 clove garlic, crushed
½ cup dry white wine
3 eggs
2 tablespoons lemon juice

METHOD

Sprinkle chicken pieces with salt, pepper and rosemary. Heat oil and brown chicken on both sides.
Cook until tender.

Stir in garlic and wine. Beat eggs with lemon juice and pour over the chicken stirring all the time. The egg must not be allowed to cook, just to thicken. Serve at once.

CHICKEN PROVENÇALE

Serves 4

INGREDIENTS

- 2 tablespoons of vegetable oil
- 1 tablespoon butter
- 1.25kg (2½lb) small chicken pieces
- 2 tablespoons brandy
- ¾ cup dry white wine
- 4 tomatoes, peeled
- 8 small onions, peeled
- 1 apple, peeled and diced
- ½ cup green olives
- 1 teaspoon curry powder
- ½ teaspoon dried thyme
- Salt to taste
- 250g (8oz) button mushrooms
- Chopped parsley
- Snipped chives

METHOD

Heat oil and butter together. Add chicken pieces and brown all over. Pour off remaining oil and butter and reserve for cooking the mushrooms. Pour brandy over chicken and flambé.

Add wine, tomatoes, onions, apple, olives, curry powder, thyme and salt. Cover with a tight-fitting lid and cook gently until tender, about 30-35 minutes, adding a little extra wine if necessary.

Cook mushrooms in the reserved oil and butter, add to chicken and sprinkle top with parsley and chives. Serve with ribbon noodles.

WARM CHICKEN SALAD

Serves 4

INGREDIENTS

- 4 boned chicken breasts
- 2 tablespoons lemon juice
- 2 tablespoons butter
- 1 cup sliced celery
- ¼ cup walnut pieces
- 2 tablespoons soft blue vein cheese
- ¼ cup French dressing
- Lettuce leaves and chives

METHOD

Place chicken breasts and lemon juice in a bowl and refrigerate for 1 hour.

Melt butter and cook chicken until golden brown. Drain and slice. Combine celery, valnuts, cheese and dressing. Arrange lettuce leaves on 4 individual plates, top with the warm chicken and then celery mixture. Sprinkle with snipped chives and serve.

Opposite page: Chicken Provençale, recipe above.

CHICKEN INDIENNE

INGREDIENTS

1 x 1.5-2kg (3-4lb) chicken
2½ cups water
2 strips lemon rind
1 onion, chopped
6 whole allspice
6 peppercorns
1 sprig thyme, 2 sprigs parsley, 1 bay leaf, tied together
1½ teaspoons salt
Sauce Inienne:
(recipe follows)

METHOD

Place chicken in heavy saucepan with water, lemon rind, onion, allspice, peppercorns, bunch of herbs and salt. Bring to boil and simmer, covered, for 45 minutes or until tender.

When cool, remove chicken from stock and take meat from bones. Discard skin and cut flesh into thick slices.

Reserve 2 cups of stock, and skim any fat from surface.

Sauce indienne: Melt 60g (2oz) butter, add 1 tablespoon curry powder and 2 tablespoons flour and stir until smooth over low heat. Cook together for a few minutes. Slowly stir in 2 cups of stock from cooked chicken and stir constantly over moderate heat until sauce thickens. Add 1 tablespoon redcurrant jelly, beating into the sauce. Allow mixture to cool, whisking once or twice. Mix in ½ cup cream, then fold in the chicken pieces and add salt and white pepper to taste. Serve cold. This dish makes an ideal part of a cold buffet, with rice and salads.

TURKEY AND MUSHROOM PIE

Serves 7-8

INGREDIENTS

90g (3oz) butter
1 onion, chopped
250g (8oz) mushrooms, sliced
¼ cup flour
Salt and pepper
1 cup chicken stock
¾ cup cream
4 cups cooked, diced turkey
250g (8oz) puff pastry

METHOD

Cook butter, onion and mushrooms until soft. Stir in flour, salt and pepper and cook 2 minutes. Add stock, cream and turkey and stir until boiling. Place in a pie dish and cover with rolled out pastry. Seal edges and make slits in top for steam to escape.

Brush with milk and bake in a hot oven 20 minutes until browned.

Following pages:
Picnic Egg and Chicken Pie, recipe above.

Emanuel Phillips Fox
1865–1915.
The Lesson 1912
Oil on canvas 182.2 x 111.8cm
Felton Bequest 1925
National Gallery of Victoria

The tray of tea things on the table and the gentle warmth of the woman and her child in this charming painting depicts a way of life that has completely disappeared. The custom of drinking tea in the afternoon was brought to the colonies by the English and became known to Australians as afternoon tea.

Because of the faster pace of modern life after the Second World War and the fact that so many women work, it declined in popularity. However, it is becoming fashionable again among those with leisure time to spare. In the past, it was a stylish ritual and to define the status of the household where an afternoon tea was held, there were fine displays of napery, silver and china. Thin bread and butter, little sandwiches, small snacks such as scones and crumpets, and cakes of all shapes and sizes provided agreeable accompaniments to tea, conversation and gossip. For Australian workers, morning and afternoon tea breaks are still essential; a cup of tea and a biscuit offer a welcome escape from routine.

EST. 1844
Penfolds
Trameah
RIESLING

CHERRIED QUAIL

Serves 4

INGREDIENTS

4 quails
4 small pieces of orange rind, with pith removed
6 tablespoons butter, approximately
4 parsley sprigs
2 small onions, halved
Fresh or dried thyme
Pork fat or bacon
Salt and pepper
⅔ cup water
½ cup dry white wine
½ cup stoned canned cherries

Bread sauce: (optional)
1 small onion, finely chopped
1 cup milk
1 bay leaf
4 peppercorns
1 cup soft white breadcrumbs
Salt
1 teaspoon butter

METHOD

Wipe the birds inside and out with paper towels. Put in the cavity of each a small piece of orange rind, about 2 teaspoons of the butter, a parsley sprig, an onion half, and a good pinch of thyme. Tie the legs and wings of each bird close to its body with string. Cover the breast of each with pork fat or bacon and tie with string. Melt 3 tablespoons of the remaining butter in a large baking dish, add the quails, and brown them all over.

Cover the dish, put in a very hot oven, and roast for 20 minutes, basting several times with the fat and juices in the dish. Remove the pork fat or bacon and the trussing string, baste the birds well, and sprinkle with salt and pepper. Lower the oven temperature to moderate and return the birds for 5 minutes. Remove the birds to a heated serving platter and keep hot while you make the gravy.

Add the water and wine to the dish and stir over brisk heat, scraping up the pan juices, for 2-3 minutes. Stir in the remaining tablespoon of butter and season with salt and pepper to taste. Add the cherries and heat through. Serve the birds with the gravy and bread sauce.

Bread sauce: Put the onion in a saucepan with the milk, bay leaf, and peppercorns.

Cook over gentle heat for 20 minutes. Strain and then mix in the breadcrumbs and salt to taste. Simmer 3-4 minutes. Stir in the butter.

PICNIC EGG AND CHICKEN PIE

Serves 8

INGREDIENTS

1 cup plain flour
1 cup self-raising flour
1 teaspoon salt
155g (5oz) butter, chopped
1 egg yolk, lightly beaten
Cold water
8 chicken breasts
1 ham steak
6 spring onions, finely chopped
1 tablespoon chopped parsley
1 teaspoon mixed dried herbs
Pepper and salt
5 hard-boiled eggs
Beaten egg yolk for glazing

METHOD

Sift the flours and salt into a mixing bowl. Rub the butter in with fingertips until mixture resembles breadcrumbs. Add the egg yolk with enough cold water to form a firm dough. Chill for about 30 minutes.

Take two-thirds and roll out to fit into a 23cm (9in) greased springform tin. Shred chicken breasts and cube the ham steak. In a bowl, mix with the spring onions, parsley, mixed herbs and pepper and salt. Spread half of the mixture into the pastry case. Arrange the whole shelled hard boiled eggs over the top and cover with the remaining mixture. Roll out the rest of the pastry to form a cover. Moisten the edges of the pastry case and place cover on top, pressing edges together to seal. Decorate with scraps, brush with beaten egg yolk. Cut two small slits in top to allow steam to escape. Bake in a moderately hot oven for 30 minutes. Reduce heat to moderate and bake a further 1 hour, covering the top with foil if it browns too quickly. Cool and chill in the refrigerator. Serve with salads.

Following pages: Turkey Tetrazzini, recipe page 168.

Ena Joyce
After Lunch 1982
Gouache 37.5 x 55cm
Bathurst Regional Art Gallery

DUCK WITH GREEN PEPPERCORNS

Serves 4

INGREDIENTS

1 x 2.5kg (4½lb) duck
Salt and pepper
2 tablespoons chopped parsley

Peppercorn sauce
1 small onion, finely chopped
4 tablespoons red wine vinegar
1 teaspoon chopped fresh tarragon or ½ teaspoon dried tarragon
1 teaspoon snipped fresh thyme or ½ teaspoon dried thyme
3 tablespoons canned green peppercorns
2 teaspoons French mustard
1½ cups stock made with duck neck and giblets, or chicken stock

METHOD

Remove excess fat from the inside of the duck. Wipe inside and outside with damp paper towels. Sprinkle salt and pepper inside. Truss the duck and put it, breast side up, on a rack in a baking dish. Roast in a moderately hot oven for 15 minutes and then prick all around the tail end to release the fat. Continue roasting for 1¾ hours, or until tender when tested, basting occasionally.

While the duck is cooking, make the sauce. Remove the duck to a heated platter and keep warm. Spoon as much fat as possible from the baking dish and discard this fat. Stir the drippings from the baking dish into the peppercorn sauce. Stir until reheated, add the parsley, and simmer for 1 minute. Carve the duck into serving portions, spoon a little of the sauce over, and serve the rest separately.

Peppercorn sauc: Put the onion in a small saucepan with the vinegar, tarragon, and thyme. Bring to the boil, stirring, then continue boiling gently until the liquid has evaporated.

Rinse the peppercorns in cold water and add to the onion with the mustard and stock. Stir until boiling, then cook gently until reduced a little.

Following pages: Duckling Nouvelle with Strawberry Coulis, recipe page 171.

TURKEY TETRAZZINI

Serves 4-5

INGREDIENTS

- 250 g (8 oz) pink, green or white tagliatelle or a mixture of all three
- 4 tablespoons butter
- 125 g (4 oz) mushrooms, thinly sliced
- 1 small onion, grated
- ¼ cup plain flour
- 1 cup evaporated milk
- 1½ cups chicken stock
- 2 tablespoons dry sherry
- Salt and pepper
- 1 small green and 1 small red capsicum, cut into short thin strips
- 2 cups diced cooked turkey
- ½ cup grated Parmesan cheese

METHOD

Cook the spaghetti in plenty of boiling salted water until tender. Drain and arrange in a greased ovenproof dish. Melt half the butter, add the mushrooms, and gently fry until softened. Add the rest of the butter and the onion and cook for 20 seconds. Stir in the flour, and cook for 1 minute. Slowly stir in the evaporated milk and the stock and cook, stirring, until boiling. Add the sherry, season with salt and pepper, and simmer for 1-2 minutes.

Drop the strips of capsicum into a small pan of cold water and slowly bring to the boil. Drain and add to the sauce. Pour half the sauce over the spaghetti, mixing in.

Add the turkey to the rest of the sauce and pour into the dish. Sprinkle with the grated cheese and bake in a moderately hot oven for about 15 minutes. Serve with a green salad.

HONEY DUCKLING

Serves 4-5

INGREDIENTS

- 1 x 2.25 kg (4½ lb) duckling
- Salt and pepper
- Grated rind 1 orange
- 2 cloves garlic, crushed
- 1 small onion, chopped finely
- 3 tablespoons soy sauce
- 3 tablespoons sherry
- 2 tablespoons honey

METHOD

Rub inside duck with salt, pepper and orange rind. Pierce all over with a skewer and bake on a rack in a baking dish in a moderate oven.

Combine all remaining ingredients and brush over duck while cooking.

Cook until tender, about 2 hours.

Opposite page: Chicken with Cheese Sauce, recipe page 170.

CHICKEN KEBABS WITH PEANUT SAUCE

Serves 4

INGREDIENTS

8 chicken liver halves
2 bacon rashers, rind removed
8 small pieces of chicken breast
8 small onions, peeled
8 tomato wedges
8 pineapple pieces
4 green capsicum strips
½ cup vegetable oil
2 tablespoons orange juice
1 tablespoon lemon juice
1 teaspoon soy sauce
1 teaspoon brown sugar
½ teaspoon ground ginger
Few drops hot pepper sauce

METHOD

Wrap the chicken livers in small pieces of the bacon and alternate on 4 skewers with all the other foods. Mix together the remaining ingredients for the marinade and brush over skewers. Grill over hot coals, or under a griller, brushing now and again with the marinade. Cook on both sides until tender. Serve with saffron rice and peanut sauce.

Peanut sauce: Mix together ½ cup sour cream, 4 tablespoons chopped salted peanuts and ½ teaspoon onion powder.

CHICKEN WITH CHEESE SAUCE

Serves 8

INGREDIENTS

2 kg (4 lb) chicken pieces
Salt and pepper
½ cup chicken stock
1 leek, sliced thinly
1 cup thickened cream
250 g (8 oz) blue vein cheese, crumbled
½ cup sour cream
¼ cup dry vermouth
½ cup walnut pieces

METHOD

Sprinkle chicken with salt and pepper and place in a baking dish.

Bake in a hot oven 25 minutes, turning once. Pour in the chicken stock, spoon over chicken and bake another 10 minutes. Place chicken in an ovenproof dish.

Place baking dish over medium heat on the stove and remove excess fat. Add leek, cream and cheese and stir until cheese melts. Simmer for a few minutes then stir in sour cream and vermouth.

Pour over the chicken and sprinkle with walnuts. Cover and bake 10 minutes.

DUCKLING NOUVELLE

Serves 2

INGREDIENTS

2 duckling breasts
2 tablespoons butter
2 tablespoons strawberry vinegar or white wine
½ cup strawberries
Black pepper
1 avocado, sliced
1 mango, sliced
1 punnet salad cress
2 tablespoons pecan nuts
Extra strawberries
Witlof leaves
1 red capsicum, peeled and cut into julienne strips
Cherry tomatoes

METHOD

Sauté duckling breasts in the butter until cooked. Put aside to cool. Skim off fat and deglaze pan with the vinegar or white wine. Strain and put in blender or food processor with ½ cup strawberries and black pepper, to form a sauce or coulis. Taste and add a little sugar if necessary. Pour a pool of coulis onto 2 plates. Slice duckling breasts into fan shapes and place beside coulis on each plate. Arrange other ingredients decoratively to form a pretty picture, using your imagination.

gredients 1 x 2.5kg (5lb) leg of lamb 90g (3oz) butter 1 medium onion,
iopped fresh rosemary (or 1/2 teaspoon dried) 2 teaspoons chopped fre
ound pepper Gravy 11/2 tablespoons plain flour 11/2 cups stock made w
one. Heat the butter and fry onion until soft and golden. Skin and cor
owned. Remove from heat and add breadcrumbs, herbs and salt and pe
ith string. Season with salt and pepper, arrange on a greased rack in
bout 2 hours for well done lamb, basting now and then with juices tha
rving.Gravy: Pour off all but 2 tablespoons of drippings in pan, and
ntinue stirring until gravy is smooth and thickened. Taste for seasonin
utter 1 medium onion, finely chopped 2 lamb kidneys 2 cups soft, white

Meat and game

y chopped 2 lamb kidneys 2 cups soft, white breadcrumbs 2 teaspoor
age (or 1/2 teaspoon dried) 2 teaspoons chopped parsley Salt and finel
lamb bone method Ask the butcher to bone the lamb for you and save th
e kidneys and cut into small dice. Add to the pan and stir until light
to taste. Allow to cool a little, then stuff lamb and tie into a neat shap
king dish, and place in a preheated moderate oven.Roast uncovered fo
lect in the pan. Allow to rest for 20 minutes before removing string an
in flour over low heat. When well blended, gradually stir in stock an
d strain into a gravy boat. ingredients 1 x 2.5kg (5lb) leg of lamb 90g (3o
adcrumbs 2 teaspoons chopped fresh rosemary (or 1/2 teaspoon dried)

TEXAS HOTPOT

Serves 2-3

INGREDIENTS

250g (8oz) thickly sliced bacon
2 onions, sliced
1 clove garlic, crushed
1 x 400g can tomatoes
4-6 small potatoes, sliced
Salt and pepper
3-4 fresh or frozen corn cobs

METHOD

Cook bacon in its own fat until browned. Remove. Add onion and garlic to bacon fat and cook a few minutes. Add a little butter if necessary.

Stir in undrained tomatoes, sliced potatoes, salt and pepper to taste and the bacon.

Cook gently with the lid on 10-15 minutes.

Slice the corn cobs and press into the hotpot, adding a small amount of vegetable stock if necessary. Cover pot and cook until corn is tender, about 10 minutes.

SPICY GLAZED PORK

Serves 4-5

INGREDIENTS

1.5kg (3lb) pork shoulder
2 teaspoons curry powder
1 teaspoon ground ginger
1 clove garlic, crushed
1 teaspoon dried thyme
Salt to taste
2 carrots, sliced
1 parsnip, sliced
1 turnip, cut into pieces
1 leek, washed and sliced
2 cups beef stock
3 teaspoons arrowroot

METHOD

Cut pork in half if desired. Combine curry, ginger, garlic, thyme and salt. Rub into pork and place in an ovenproof dish.

Place the vegetables around the meat and pour over the stock. Cover with lid and bake in a moderate oven until meat is tender.

Carefully pour the stock into a saucepan, stir in blended arrowroot and cook until boiling and thickened. Pour over meat in dish and serve.

Opposite page: Texas Hotpot, recipe above.

VENISON WITH WALNUTS

Serves 6-8

INGREDIENTS

- 1kg (2lb) stewing venison (cut from shoulder)
- 2 tablespoons plain flour
- 1 teaspoon dried mixed herbs
- 2 medium onions, finely chopped
- 2 large tomatoes, peeled and chopped
- Salt and freshly ground pepper
- Small piece cinnamon stick
- 5 pickled walnuts, sliced
- 2 teaspoons Angostura bitters
- ¾ cup red wine
- Extra walnut slices and chopped parsley to garnish

METHOD

Remove any sinews from venison, cut meat into cubes and roll lightly in flour.

Arrange the cubes in a greased ovenproof dish in layers, sprinkling each layer with herbs, onions and tomatoes and seasoning with salt and pepper as you go.

Add the cinnamon stick and pickled walnut slices. Combine bitters and red wine and pour into the dish. Cover tightly and cook in a moderate oven for 1½ - 2 hours or until venison is fork tender. Serve topped with a few pickled walnut slices and chopped parsley.

VEAL CORDON BLEU

Serves 4

INGREDIENTS

- 4 thin veal steaks
- 2 tablespoons vegetable oil
- Salt
- French mustard
- 4 ham slices
- 4 slices Swiss or Emmenthal cheese

METHOD

Cook veal steaks in hot oil for 1 minute on each side. Remove and place on grilling tray. Sprinkle with salt to taste and spread with mustard. Cover with a slice of ham, then with a slice of cheese.

Grill under high heat until cheese is bubbly and golden.

MEATBALLS WITH GREEN PEPPERCORN SAUCE

Serves 4

INGREDIENTS

500g (1lb) minced beef
1 egg
½ cup soft breadcrumbs
1 tablespoon French mustard
Salt and pepper to taste
3 tablespoons vegetable oil
185g (6oz) fresh mushrooms, sliced
1 x 25g packet brown sauce mix
1¼ cups evaporated milk
1 tablespoon dry sherry
2 tablespoons green peppercorns
Chopped parsley

METHOD

Mix together minced beef, egg, breadcrumbs, mustard, salt and pepper and form into balls.

Heat oil, add meatballs and brown all over, shaking pan frequently. Add mushrooms and continue cooking until meatballs are cooked.

Make up the sauce mix with evaporated milk, stir in sherry and peppercorns.

Pour over meatballs and sprinkle with chopped parsley.

VEAL ESCALOPES WITH SMOKED HAM

Serves 4-6

INGREDIENTS

6 thin veal steaks
Salt and pepper
1-2 tablespoons chopped fresh sage
6 slices smoked ham
Flour
60g (2oz) butter
½ cup rosé or light white wine

METHOD

Season meat with salt and pepper and sprinkle evenly with sage. Place a slice of ham on each veal steak and fasten with a wooden toothpick. Coat lightly in flour.

Cook slowly in the butter. Pour over the wine and stir vigorously to combine with the butter. Remove picks and serve with sautÈed potatoes.

Rosella
TOMATO
PLAZA
3 BIG STARS BRING YOU
Together for the first time in an enthralling ★ love story— a perfect romance!
CLARK GABLE
CLAUDETTE COLBERT IN
It Happened One Night
TALLY-HO
50 GUMMED PAPERS
MADE IN GREAT BRITAIN

AUSSIE MEAT PIES

Serves 4

INGREDIENTS

250g (8oz) shortcrust pastry
1 tablespoon butter
1 onion, finely chopped
250g (8oz) minced beef
1 tablespoon plain flour
2 tablespoons tomato sauce
1 tablespoon Worcestershire sauce
2 tablespoons water
Salt and pepper
Beaten egg for glazing

METHOD

Roll pastry out thinly, cut into rounds and line four 10 cm (4 in) pie tins.

Meanwhile make filling. Heat the butter and gently fry the onion until transparent. Add beef and stir until browned. Stir in flour, sauces, water, salt and pepper, and bring to boil. Remove from heat and cool. Divide filling between the 4 tins, cut 4 rounds from remaining pastry and cover each pie, crimping edges. Make a vent with a skewer in the centre of each and decorate with pastry trimmings. Brush with beaten egg. Stand tins on a baking tray and bake in a hot oven 20 minutes until cooked.

Serve with tomato sauce or, for a more substantial meal, with creamy mashed potatoes and peas.

The meat pie came to us from England and ultimately became a popular commercial food favourite here. The pie with tomato sauce is sometimes called our national dish.

Its portability lends extra charm to its often dubious contents. Homemade meat pies were sold in the streets of Sydney and Melbourne in the very early days. During the Depression a few shillings would pay for a pie and a picture show. Our Aussie Meat Pie, recipe above, is a version of the classic original and offers the flavours and succulent textures which have made it so popular for so long.

STEAK AND OYSTER PIE

Serves 6

INGREDIENTS

1kg (2lb) chuck steak, fat removed, cubed
375g (12oz) ox kidney, skin and fat removed, chopped
Flour seasoned with salt and pepper
60g (2oz) butter
2 onions, chopped
1¼ cups beef stock
½ teaspoon dried thyme
Salt and pepper
Dash of Worcestershire sauce
1 tablespoon chopped parsley
2 dozen fresh oysters
375g (12oz) puff pastry
Egg yolk or milk for glazing

METHOD

Lightly coat the steak and kidney pieces with seasoned flour. In a large wide heavy saucepan, brown all over in the heated butter. Add the onions and cook 2-3 minutes, stirring. Pour off fat, add beef stock and stir until nearly boiling. Add the thyme, salt, pepper and Worcestershire sauce. Cook gently about 1 ½ hours or until meat is almost tender.

Mix in parsley. Transfer to a pie dish and put aside. When cold, add the oysters.

Roll out the pastry to an oblong a little larger than the dish, cut narrow strips from ends. Moisten edges of pie dish, top with pastry strips. Brush with water and top with rest of the pastry. Press edges together, trim off excess. Make 2 or 3 slits in top and decorate with pastry trimmings. Brush over with beaten egg yolk or milk. Bake in a very hot oven for 15 minutes, reduce to moderate and bake another 20-25 minutes.

CRUSTY LEG OF LAMB

Serves 6

INGREDIENTS

- 1 x 1.5-2kg (3-4lb) leg lamb
- 1 egg yolk
- 3 tablespoons butter, melted
- 1 cup cornflake crumbs
- 1 tablespoon sesame seeds
- Salt to taste
- ½ teaspoon seasoned mixed herbs
- 1 small onion, sliced

METHOD

Remove excess fat from lamb, brush top of surface with a little of the egg yolk.

Mix together butter, cornflake crumbs, sesame seeds, salt, seasoned mixed herbs and half the remaining egg yolk.

Press mixture firmly over top of lamb, break onion slices into rings and arrange in a pattern over the crumb surface, pressing with the palm of your hand. Brush the onion rings with rest of egg yolk.

Put into a baking dish and bake in a moderate oven about 1½ hours, or until done to your liking. When the crust becomes golden and crisp, cover with foil for the rest of the cooking time.

RICE AND SAUSAGE CASSEROLE

Serves 6

INGREDIENTS

- 500g (1lb) sausages oil
- 1 large onion finely chopped
- 1 small green capsicum, diced
- 3 large tomatoes, peeled and chopped
- 1½ cups long-grain rice
- 3 mushroom stock-cubes, crumbled
- 3 cups hot water
- salt and pepper
- 1 cup cooked green peas

METHOD

Put the sausages in a saucepan with enough cold water to cover and slowly bring to the boil. Rinse in cold water and drain thoroughly.

Heat oil and brown sausages quickly all over. Drain on paper towels and cut crossways into quarters.

Heat a little more oil and fry the onion gently in the pan until softened. Add the capsicum and tomatoes and cook, stirring, for 2or 3 minutes. Add the sausage sections and the rice, stirring well.

Transfer to an oven proof dish. Dissolve the stock-cubes in hot water and pour into the dish. Add salt and pepper, cover with a tight-fitting lid, and cook in a moderately hot oven for 25 minutes, or until the liquid has been absorbed and the rice is tender. Add the green peas, mixing it with a fork, and return to the oven for 5 minutes.

RABBIT TERRINE

Serves 8

INGREDIENTS

- Meat from back legs and saddles of 2 rabbits, minced and marinated a few hours in ¼ cup brandy
- 2 rabbit or chicken livers, finely chopped
- 500g (1lb) streaky pork belly, minced
- 1 white onion, finely chopped and sauteed in 1 tablespoon butter
- 125g (4oz) chopped mushrooms
- 1 teaspoon chopped fresh rosemary
- 1 teaspoon chopped parsley
- ½ cup white wine
- Salt and pepper
- ½ teaspoon ground nutmeg
- 2 tablespoons cream
- 2 bay leaves
- 6 rashers bacon, rinds removed

METHOD

In a bowl combine all ingredients except bay leaves and bacon. Line an ovenproof terrine with the bacon, leaving ends of rashers overlapping sides. Fill terrine with mixture.

Place bay leaves on top and bring overlapping bacon ends over top. Bake in a baking dish half full of water in a moderate oven 1 - 1¼ hours or until juices run clear when tested with skewer. Serve with salad, Herb Toasts and a jug of Sangria, a refreshing Spanish drink.

Herb toast: French bread slices, rubbed with crushed garlic, brushed with olive oil sprinkled with fresh or dried mixed herbs of your choice. Arrange on a baking tray and in moderate oven until golden and crisp. They will keep well in an airtight container.

SANGRIA

INGREDIENTS

- 1½ cups water
- 1 cup sugar
- 1 cinnamon stick
- 2 lemons, sliced
- 1 bottle red wine
- Soda water
- Ice
- Mint leaves

METHOD

Place water, sugar and cinnamon stick in a saucepan and stir until boiling and sugar is dissolved. Simmer 5 minutes.

Place lemon slices in a bowl and pour over the syrup. Allow to stand for a few hours.

Stir in the wine, soda water to taste, ice and mint leaves. Pour into a jug and serve in wine glasses.

Following pages: Rabbit Terrine with salad, Herb Toasts and Sangria, recipes above.

CHINESE BEEF AND VEGETABLES

Serves 8

INGREDIENTS

3 tablespoons vegetable oil
1kg (2lb) lean beef, cut into thin strips
125g (4oz) mushrooms, sliced
1 carrot, cut into thin strips
1 x 230g can water chestnuts, drained
6 shallots, cut into strips
1 large capsicum, cut into strips
1 cup thin strips of celery
250g (8oz) bean sprouts
3 garlic cloves, crushed
2 tablespoons chopped fresh ginger
1 cup chicken stock
1 tablespoon soy sauce
2 tablespoons dry sherry
3 teaspoons arrowroot or cornflour

METHOD

Heat oil. Brown meat and mushrooms quickly. Remove. Add carrot, water chestnuts, shallots, capsicum, celery, bean sprouts, garlic and ginger and stir-fry lightly.

Mix remaining ingredients together, and add to pan, together with meat and mushrooms. Stir until thickened and clear. Serve with rice.

LAMB BURGERS

Serves 4

INGREDIENTS

500g (1lb) minced lamb
1 onion, grated
½ cup soft breadcrumbs
2 tablespoons chopped parsley
1 egg
1 clove garlic, crushed
Salt and pepper to taste
2 tablespoons oil

METHOD

Combine minced lamb with all ingredients and form into fairly large burgers.

Heat oil and cook on both sides until browned. Cook until tender. Burgers should be pink on the inside.

Opposite page: Chinese Beef and Vegetables, recipe above.

1979
Chianti
Melini

VEAL ESCALOPES WITH GORGONZOLA SAUCE

Serves 4-6

INGREDIENTS

6 thin veal steaks
Salt and pepper
Flour
2 tablespoons butter
90g (3oz) Gorgonzola cheese
1 tablespoon butter
1 tablespoon brandy
½ cup cream

METHOD

Season veal with salt and pepper and dip lightly into flour. Melt the 2 tablespoons butter and cook veal on both sides until lightly browned. Keep warm.

Stir cheese and the 1 tablespoon butter together until cheese melts then add brandy and stir well. Add cream and heat gently. Strain if necessary and pour over the veal steaks.

BEEF IN RED WINE

Serves 4

INGREDIENTS

1kg (2lb) piece of roasting beef
Salt and pepper
2 tablespoons oil
2 carrots, sliced
2 onions, cut into wedges
1 cup diced celery
2 cloves garlic, crushed
2 tablespoons flour
2 cups red wine
2 peeled tomatoes, chopped

METHOD

Sprinkle beef with salt and pepper and brown on all sides in the hot oil. Add carrots, onion, celery and garlic and cook a few minutes.

Sprinkle flour over the top, stir in and cook 2-3 minutes. Add wine and tomatoes.

Cover and bake in a moderate oven until tender, about 1 ½ hours.

Continental restaurants, bistros and street cafés proliferated after the Second World War. Scenes, such as the one opposite became commonplace in our cities, and Italian cuisine has always been popular. Top, Veal Escalopes with Smoked Ham, recipe page 177; right, Veal Escalopes with Gorgonzola Sauce, recipe above; below, Italian Lemon Chicken, recipe page 152.

STEAK WITH PEARS

Serves 2

INGREDIENTS

2 T-bone steaks
4 canned pear halves
Melted butter
Ground ginger

Marinade:
¼ cup honey
¼ cup soy sauce
Juice of 1 medium lemon
1 cup tomato sauce
Pepper

METHOD

About 1¼ hours before the steaks are needed, put them in a shallow dish and spoon the marinade over. Turn the steaks once while they are marinating. Just before cooking, remove and drain the steaks. Grill until cooked to your liking.

While the steaks are grilling, brush the pear halves with melted butter, sprinkle with ginger, and heat through in a moderately hot oven, or under the griller. Gently heat the marinade and serve with the meat.

Marinade: Mix together the honey, soy sauce, lemon juice, tomato sauce and pepper to taste.

DEVILLED PORK CHOPS

Serves 4

INGREDIENTS

4 loin pork chops
Salt and pepper
6 shallots, chopped
1 tablespoon green peppercorns
1 cup red wine

METHOD

Season chops with salt and pepper and cook quickly on both sides until lightly browned.

Add shallots and cook a few minutes. Stir in peppercorns and wine and cook gently until reduced by half.

Taste for seasoning and serve at once with cooked vegetables.

Margaret Preston 1875–1963
The Snail 1949
Gouache stencil on black card
29.9 x 21.2cm
purchased 1949
Art Gallery of New South Wales

GOLD COAST RACK OF LAMB

Serves 6

INGREDIENTS

2 racks of lamb, each with 6 cutlets
½ cup redcurrant jelly
2 tablespoons pineapple juice
1 teaspoon salt
¼ teaspoon pepper

Seasoning:
2 tablespoons butter
1 cup coarse soft wholemeal breadcrumbs
1 cup fresh or canned chopped pineapple with juice
1½ tablespoons chopped mint
Salt and pepper
½ teaspoon ground or 1 teaspoon finely chopped fresh ginger

Redcurrant Mint Sauce:
1 tablespoon redcurrant jelly dissolved with 1 tablespoon boiling water
2 tablespoons red wine vinegar
2 tablespoons finely chopped mint

METHOD

Remove the fine skin from the fat on the lamb and place the racks on a baking dish, fat side up. Melt the redcurrant jelly and pineapple juice over hot water, season with salt and pepper and brush over cutlets. Bake in a moderately hot oven for 25 minutes.

Remove from oven and brush again with glaze. Return to oven and continue baking until done to your liking.

Make gravy in the usual way, using vegetable stock for liquid. Bake seasoning in oven on a separate greased pie dish.

Seasoning: Heat the butter and toss breadcrumbs in it until they are golden brown.

Mix lightly with pineapple, mint, salt, pepper and ginger. Place in dish and cover lightly with foil, removing foil towards end of cooking. Remove from oven and keep warm until ready to serve with cutlets. Hand Redcurrant Mint Sauce separately.

Red currant mint sauce: Mix ingredients together, adding extra jelly, hot water or vinegar to taste.

Opposite page: Gold Coast Rack of Lamb with Pineapple Seasoning, recipe above.

x 425g can whole peeled tomatoes, chopped, and their liquid Chicken s
f garlic, crushed 1 medium green capsicum, diced 2 cups long grain ric
ooked ham, diced 250g (8oz) prawns, peeled and deveined 2 breasts of co
nd their liquid and add enough stock to make 3 cups. Heat gently un
apsicum, and fry gently for 1-2 minutes. Add the rice and stir over low
e ham. Add the boiling tomato mixture, cover tightly, and cook over low
dding a little more stock if necessary. Scatter the prawns and chicken c
eated through. Sprinkle with Tabasco and chopped parsley, and serve.
reshly ground black pepper 1 tablespoon chopped parsley 4 slices of co
hicken, diced Tabasco Chopped parsley method Measure the tomatoes

Pasta & rice

or water 3 tablespoons butter or oil 1 large onion, finely chopped 1 clo
lt Freshly ground black pepper 1 tablespoon chopped parsley 4 slices
l chicken, diced Tabasco Chopped parsley method Measure the tomato
oiling. Heat the butter or oil in a large pan, add the onion, garlic, ar
for 2-3 minutes. Mix in salt and black pepper to taste, the parsley, ar
at for 20 minutes, or until the rice is tender and liquid has been absorbe
the top, replace the lid, and return to very low heat until the prawns a
lic, crushed 1 medium green capsicum, diced 2 cups long grain rice Sa
l ham, diced 250g (8oz) prawns, peeled and deveined 2 breasts of cooke
d their liquid and add enough stock to make 3 cups. Heat gently unt

LAMB PILAF

Serves 4

INGREDIENTS

500g (1lb) boneless lamb, diced
90g (3oz) ghee or butter
1 onion, chopped
1 carrot, cut into julienne strips
Salt and pepper
2 cups uncooked rice
3½ cups boiling chicken stock
½ cup raisins
Sliced raw onion
Chopped parsley

METHOD

Brown meat in the ghee or butter. Stir in onion and carrot and cook for a few minutes.

Season to taste with salt and pepper, add rice and stir until coated with ghee.

Pour over the boiling stock, cover with a tight-fitting lid and cook until rice is tender and liquid has been absorbed, about 20 minutes. Add raisins, replace lid and leave until plumped.

Garnish with onion slices and chopped parsley and serve.

TAGLIATELLE WITH MUSSELS

Serves 4 entrées

INGREDIENTS

1kg (2lb) mussels
¼ cup olive oil
1 tablespoon butter
4 tomatoes, peeled
1 clove garlic, crushed
1 onion, chopped finely
Salt and pepper
1 tablespoon chopped fresh basil
500g (1lb) tagliatelle, cooked
Thin strips shallots or zucchini for garnish

METHOD

Wash mussels well and cook in the hot oil until shells have opened. Keep a few for garnish and remove the remaining mussels from their shells. Strain liquid from mussels and reserve. Melt butter, add chopped tomatoes, garlic and onion and cook a few minutes. Stir in mussel liquid and season with salt and pepper to taste. Lastly stir in basil.

Place the hot drained tagliatelle on individual plates. Spoon tomato mixture on top, add the warm mussels in their sheets and garnish with fine strips of shallot or zucchini.

Opposite page: Lamb Pilaf, recipe above.

NOODLES WITH FRESH TOMATO SAUCE

Serves 4

INGREDIENTS

2 onions, chopped
1 cup chopped celery or zucchini
2 tablespoons butter
750g (1½lb) ripe tomatoes, peeled
3 tablespoons tomato paste
1 vegetable stock cube
1 tablespoon chopped fresh basil
½ cup grated Parmesan cheese
1 cup thick cream
500g (1lb) ribbon noodles

METHOD

Sauté onions and celery in the butter for a few minutes. Stir in chopped tomatoes, tomato paste, crumbled stock cube and the basil. Add a little water if necessary and simmer to a rich thick sauce.

Taste for seasoning and add salt and pepper if necessary. Gently heat the cheese and cream together, mix with the hot, drained noodles. Serve in deep plates with the tomato sauce spooned on the top.

PASTA WITH HERBS

Serves 4 Appetisers

INGREDIENTS

8-10 lasagne sheets
1 tablespoon vegetable oil
½ cup chopped parsley
¼ cup chopped fresh basil
⅓ cup water
2 tablespoons butter
½ cup grated Parmesan cheese

METHOD

Cook lasagne sheets in boiling salted water with the oil until tender.

Mix parsley and basil together. Heat water, stir in butter until melted and add parsley and basil.

Drain lasagne, place on individual plates, sprinkle with Parmesan and pour over the herb sauce.

Opposite page: Noodles with Fresh Tomato Sauce, recipe above.

JAMBALAYA

Serves 4-5

INGREDIENTS

1 x 425g can whole peeled tomatoes, chopped, and their liquid
Chicken stock or water
3 tablespoons butter or oil
1 large onion, finely chopped
1 clove of garlic, crushed
1 medium green capsicum, diced
2 cups long grain rice
Salt
Freshly ground black pepper
1 tablespoon chopped parsley
4 slices of cooked ham, diced
250g (8oz) prawns, peeled and deveined
2 breasts of cooked chicken, diced
Tabasco
Chopped parsley

METHOD

Measure the tomatoes and their liquid and add enough stock to make 3 cups. Heat gently until boiling. Heat the butter or oil in a large pan, add the onion, garlic, and capsicum, and fry gently for 1-2 minutes. Add the rice and stir over low heat for 2-3 minutes. Mix in salt and black pepper to taste, the parsley, and the ham. Add the boiling tomato mixture, cover tightly, and cook over low heat for 20 minutes, or until the rice is tender and liquid has been absorbed, adding a little more stock if necessary.

Scatter the prawns and chicken over the top, replace the lid, and return to very low heat until the prawns are heated through. Sprinkle with Tabasco and chopped parsley, and serve.

NOODLES WITH ROQUEFORT

Serves 4 entrées

INGREDIENTS

500g (1lb) broccoli
2 tablespoons butter
2 cloves garlic, finely chopped
500g (1lb) ribbon noodles, cooked
90g (3oz) Roquefort

METHOD

Divide broccoli into small heads and cook in boiling salted water until still crisp. Melt butter, add garlic and cook very gently until softened, but not brown. Toss the hot cooked noodles with the garlic butter and place on individual serving plates together with the drained broccoli. Crumble the Roquefort over the top.

KEDGEREE

Serves 5

INGREDIENTS

½ cup long grain rice
500g (1lb) smoked cod or haddock
1 egg
2 tablespoons cream
3 tablespoons butter
2 hard-boiled eggs, roughly chopped
2 teaspoons curry powder
1 tablespoon chopped parsley

METHOD

Cook the rice in boiling salted water for about 12 minutes; drain thoroughly.

Poach the fish in water until tender; drain, remove skin and bones, and flake.

Beat the egg with the cream. Melt the butter in a large saucepan. Stir in the rice, fish, chopped eggs, and the curry powder. Stir, using a fork, until very hot. Remove from the heat, add the egg and cream, and mix well. Serve sprinkled with the chopped parsley.

PASTA WITH MOZZARELLA

Serves 4

INGREDIENTS

8 zucchini
4 cloves garlic, thinly sliced
60g (2oz) butter
Salt to taste
Freshly ground pepper
500g (1lb) spaghetti, cooked
185g (6oz) mozarella, sliced thinly

METHOD

Cut zucchini lengthwise into thin julienne strips. Cook with the garlic in the butter for a few minutes.

Drain the hot cooked spaghetti and toss with the zucchini mixture. Season with salt and pepper. Place in serving bowls, add the cheese and let it soften. Serve with salad.

tablespoons butter 1/2 cup plain flour 1/2 teaspoon salt 2 cups milk 4 e
g (3oz) Swiss cheese, shredded Swiss cheese sauce: 90g (3oz) butter 1/
eese, shredded method Lightly grease a 37 x 25 x 2 cm (15 x 10 x 1 in,
our. Melt the butter in a saucepan. Stir in the flour and salt and cook
ilk. Return to the heat and cook, stirring constantly, until very thick. B
owly beat the sauce mixture into the yolks until blended. Fold in the
inutes, or until the top is golden and springs back when touched lightl
e hot broccoli and three-quarters of the cheese on top; pour over ha
atter. Pour the remaining sauce over and sprinkle with the rest of the
saucepan. Add the flour, salt and pepper. Stir constantly over low

Vegetables and salads

eparated 1 x 238g packet of frozen broccoli cooked, drained and choppe
plain flour 1/2 teaspoon salt Pinch of pepper 3 cups milk 90g (3oz) Swi
ss roll tin; line with greaseproof paper, grease the paper, and dust wit
a few minutes, stirring constantly. Remove from the heat and stir in th
r 1 minute. Beat the egg whites until stiff. Beat the egg yolks until cream
n egg whites. Pour into the prepared tin. Bake in a moderate oven for
h the fingertip. Carefully turn out of the tin and peel off the paper. Spoo
e cheese sauce. Roll up, Swiss-roll fashion. Transfer the roll to a servin
ese. Cut into thick slices to serve. Swiss cheese sauce: Melt the butter
Gradually add the milk and continue cooking, stirring until the sauc

WALNUT AVOCADO SALAD

Serves 4

INGREDIENTS

Assorted lettuce leaves
3-4 small ripe avocados
½ cup walnut pieces
2 teaspoons white wine vinegar
1 teaspoon French mustard
Salt and pepper to taste
2 tablespoons walnut oil
½ cup raisins

METHOD

Arrange lettuce leaves on individual serving plates. Peel avocados and cut into slices.

Sprinkle over the walnuts.

Beat together vinegar, mustard, salt and pepper. Add oil a drop at a time, beating continuously so that the dressing is thick. Add raisins, pour over avocado and serve.

CRUNCHY CUCUMBER SALAD

Serves 4

INGREDIENTS

1 large green cucumber
1 cup chopped shallots
1 tablespoon chopped fresh mint
2 teaspoons chopped fresh basil
¼ cup sultanas
½ cup chopped walnuts
1 cup natural yoghurt
½ teaspoon salt

METHOD

Slice or chop cucumber into pieces and combine with all other ingredients.

Chill thoroughly, place in salad bowl and serve.

MUSHROOMS À LA GREQUE

Serves 4

INGREDIENTS

500g (1lb) small mushrooms, wiped with a damp cloth
1 tablespoon lemon juice
1 clove of garlic, crushed
1 tablespoon chopped parsley
2 medium tomatoes, peeled and chopped
1 tablespoon tomato paste
½ cup water
Pinch of dried oregano
Salt
Freshly ground black pepper
½ cup thinly sliced celery
1 bay leaf
¼ cup olive oil

METHOD

Trim the stems off the mushrooms. Put the lemon juice in a saucepan with the garlic, parsley, tomatoes, tomato paste, and water. Bring to the boil, stirring. Add the mushrooms, oregano, salt and black pepper to taste, the celery, bay leaf, and olive oil. Cover and simmer for 8-10 minutes. Cool and then chill in the refrigerator.

RATATOUILLE

Serves 4

INGREDIENTS

1 small eggplant
Salt to taste
2-3 tablespoons olive oil
500g (1lb) zucchini, sliced
2 onions, sliced
1 red capsicum, sliced
500g (1lb) tomatoes, chopped
1 clove garlic, crushed
2 tablespoons chopped parsley
Salt and freshly ground black pepper

METHOD

Cut eggplant into slices. Place in a colander. Sprinkle with salt and leave one hour.

Rinse and pat dry.

Heat oil in a heavy frypan. Add eggplant, sliced zucchini, onions and capsicum and cook a few minutes. Add tomatoes, garlic, parsley, salt and pepper to taste. Cover with a tight-fitting lid and cook a little longer until vegetables are tender but crisp.

Do not overcook. Serve by itself or with pasta dishes.

STUFFED VEGETABLES

Serves 3-6

INGREDIENTS

- 3 large well-shaped capsicums
- 1 tablespoon butter
- 1 medium onion, finely chopped
- 1 clove garlic, crushed
- ¼ teaspoon dried basil
- 1 tablespoon tomato paste
- ¼ cup cream
- 1 egg, beaten
- 2 tablespoons wheatgerm
- Salt and pepper
- Pinch of sugar
- 1 x 250g (8oz) can 3-bean mix, drained
- ½ cup small shell macaroni, cooked and drained
- ½ cup grated Parmesan cheese

METHOD

Cut the capsicums in halves lengthwise, remove seeds and core and blanch in boiling water 2 minutes. Refresh under cold running water and drain.

Melt the butter in a small saucepan and fry the onion, garlic and basil until onion is transparent. Remove from heat and mix in the tomato paste, cream, egg, wheatgerm, salt, pepper and sugar. Stir in the beans and shell macaroni. Spoon into the capsicums, sprinkle with cheese and bake in a moderate oven 15-20 minutes or until capsicums are tender.

Zucchini, eggplant and tomatoes may be filled and baked in the same way, but eggplant and tomatoes do not need blanching.

MELON SALAD

Serves 4-5

INGREDIENTS

- ½ honeydew melon, peeled and diced
- 1 cup seedless green grapes
- 1 cup diced pineapple
- 2 peaches, peeled and diced
- 2 apples, peeled and diced
- 1 cup sliced celery
- Shredded lettuce

METHOD

Combine melon, grapes, pineapple, peaches, apples and celery. Place half in a salad bowl. Add a layer of shredded lettuce. Cover with remaining fruit mixture.

Chill thoroughly before serving and serve with salad dressing – either a little poured over top or separately.

Pumpkin Scone Wedge, recipe page 249 and Stuffed Vegetables, recipe page 226, are two appetising examples

BROCCOLI ROULADE

Serves 6

INGREDIENTS

4 tablespoons butter
½ cup plain flour
½ teaspoon salt
2 cups milk
4 eggs, separated
1 x 238g packet of frozen broccoli cooked, drained and chopped
90g (3oz) Swiss cheese, shredded

Swiss cheese sauce:
90g (3oz) butter
½ cup plain flour
½ teaspoon salt
Pinch of pepper
3 cups milk
90g (3oz) Swiss cheese, shredded

METHOD

Lightly grease a 37 x 25 x 2 cm (15 x 10 x 1 in) Swiss roll tin; line with greaseproof paper, grease the paper, and dust with flour. Melt the butter in a saucepan. Stir in the flour and salt and cook for a few minutes, stirring constantly. Remove from the heat and stir in the milk. Return to the heat and cook, stirring constantly, until very thick.

Boil for 1 minute. Beat the egg whites until stiff. Beat the egg yolks until creamy. Slowly beat the sauce mixture into the yolks until blended. Fold in the beaten egg whites. Pour into the prepared tin. Bake in a moderate oven for 45 minutes, or until the top is golden and springs back when touched lightly with the fingertip. Carefully turn out of the tin and peel off the paper.

Spoon the hot broccoli and three-quarters of the cheese on top; pour over half the cheese sauce. Roll up, Swiss-roll fashion. Transfer the roll to a serving platter. Pour the remaining sauce over and sprinkle with the rest of the cheese.

Cut into thick slices to serve.

Swiss cheese sauce: Melt the butter in a saucepan. Add the flour, salt and pepper. Stir constantly over low heat. Gradually add the milk and continue cooking, stirring until the sauce thickens. Boil for 1 minute and then stir in the cheese.

Stir until cheese has melted.

The health food movement which swept into Australia during the early 20th century has settled into our national cuisine. The fact that fresh, wholesome often purely vegetarian food can be as delicious as any other if it is tastefully prepared has captured the imagination of many people who base their diet on fruit, vegetables, pulses and grains.

SWEET POTATO PURÉE

Serves 6

INGREDIENTS

5 large sweet potatoes, coarsely chopped
3 Granny Smith apples, peeled, cored, chopped
½ cup evaporated milk, heated
2 tablespoons melted butter
Pinch of nutmeg (optional)
Salt and pepper

METHOD

Cook the potatoes in boiling salted water until tender; drain thoroughly. Cook the apples gently in ½ cup water until tender; drain well. Purée the potatoes and apples in a blender, then transfer to a bowl. Add the hot evaporated milk, the melted butter and nutmeg, seasoning with salt and pepper to taste. Whisk until smooth, then pile into a warmed serving bowl. This is good with roast veal, lamb, pork or chicken, and with pork chops.

LUNCHEON BOUQUET

Serves 4

INGREDIENTS

125g (4oz) mushrooms
1 tablespoon lemon juice
Endive or lettuce of your choice
8 canned asparagus spears
1 ripe avocado, sliced
1 cup sliced celery
2 hard-boiled eggs, quartered
½ cup thinly sliced cucumber
1 small Spanish onion, sliced thinly
½ cup pecans
2 cups cooked brown rice, chilled
1 punnet cherry tomatoes

Horseradish dressing:
¼ cup whole egg mayonnaise
3 tablespoons cream
1 teaspoon horseradish cream

METHOD

Slice mushrooms and sprinkle with the lemon juice. Arrange endive on 4 salad plates with asparagus spears and sliced avocado. Combine celery, hard-boiled eggs, cucumber, onion, pecans, rice, tomatoes and mushrooms. Pile onto salad plates chill thoroughly. Combine Dressing ingredients and pour over salad just before serving.

Serve with crusty bread.

x 100g block cooking chocolate 125g (4oz) butter 2 cups brown sugar 1 tea
carbonate of soda 3/4 cup sour cream 1/2 cup boiling water Butter
ablespoons sherry or cherry brandy 1/2 cup chopped glacé cherries Ch
ater. Beat together butter, sugar and vanilla essence until creamy. A
hocolate. Mix in sifted dry ingredients alternately with sour cream and
aper-lined 20 cm (8 in) sandwich cake tins and bake in a moderate oven
minutes before removing cake tins. These cakes are soft and delicate s
nd join the 3 layers together. Cover top and sides with the remainder,

Desserts & cakes

oon vanilla essence 3 eggs 2 cups self-raising flour Pinch salt 1/2 teaspoo
eam filling and frosting: 250g (8oz) butter 4 cups icing sugar, sifted
ed walnuts Whole maraschino cherries method Melt chocolate over h
eggs one at a time and beat well after each addition. Beat in melte
iling water and beat until smooth. Divide evenly into 3 greased and ba
proximately 30 minutes until cooked. Invert onto cake coolers and lea
andle carefully. Mix the glacé cherries into a quarter of the butter crea
erving some for piping on the top. Spread smoothly and press choppe

PAVLOVA CROWN

INGREDIENTS

6 egg whites
1¾ cups caster sugar
2 teaspoons cornflour
1 teaspoon vinegar
1 teaspoon vanilla essence
1½ cups cream, whipped
1 tablespoon icing sugar, sifted
Pulp 3-4 passionfruit
Strawberries
Mulberries

METHOD

Beat egg whites until stiff peaks form. Add sugar gradually, beating on high speed on electric mixer until thick and glossy. Fold in cornflour, vinegar and vanilla essence.

Spread three-quarters of the mixture onto an oven tray lined with baking paper and shape into an oblong. Spoon the remaining meringue mixture into small mounds onto baking paper lined oven trays.

Bake both in a slow oven about 1 hour until lightly coloured and crisp.

Remove from oven and cool.

Mix cream and icing sugar together and spread over the oblong base. Press the small meringues into the cream around the edge.

Cover cream with passionfruit and decorate with strawberries and mulberries.

MANGO JELLY

Serves 4-5

INGREDIENTS

1 large ripe mango
2 tablespoons sherry
¼ cup orange juice
1 tablespoon lemon juice
¼ cup icing sugar, sifted
3 teaspoons gelatine
¾ cup thickened cream, whipped
Papaw, melon wedges, kiwi fruit and passionfruit, for decoration

METHOD

Peel mango, cut flesh from stone and pulverise in a processor. Tip into a basin and stir in sherry, orange and lemon juice, and icing sugar.

Soften gelatine in a little cold water and stir over hot water until dissolved. Cool.

Fold into mango mixture together with whipped cream.

Pour into a wet or lightly oiled 4-cup mould and chill until set. Unmould onto a serving platter and surround with papaw and melon wedges, sliced kiwi fruit and passionfruit.

Some cynics have said that the pavlova was originally created in New Zealand. Nevertheless, this delectable meringue dessert traditionally filled with whipped cream and fruit, has settled into the Australian cuisine as one of its most popular dishes. The creamy filling can be flavoured with liqueur, vanilla, chocolate or lemon, combined with glacé, canned or fresh fruits. This version, called Pavlova Crown, recipe page 212, is decorated with a ring of small meringues and garnished with passionfruit and berries.

Opposite page: Mango Jelly, recipe above. Following page: Pavlova Crown with Passionfruit and Berries.

SOLDIER'S CHRISTMAS CAKE

INGREDIENTS

250g (8oz) seeded raisins, chopped
250g (8oz) sultanas
250g (8oz) currants
125g (4oz) glacé cherries, chopped
125g (4oz) chopped mixed peel
125g (4oz) blanched almonds, chopped
⅔ cup brandy or orange juice
2 cups plain flour
½ cup self-raising flour
Pinch of salt
½ teaspoon nutmeg
½ teaspoon cinnamon
1 teaspoon mixed spice
250g (8oz) butter
1½ cups brown sugar
2 tablespoons dark jam or marmalade
4 eggs

METHOD

Mix the seeded raisins with the sultanas, currants, cherries, mixed peel, and almonds.

Sprinkle with the brandy or orange juice.

Sift the flours with the salt and spices. Beat the butter and brown sugar until light and fluffy. Add the jam and beat again. Add the eggs, one at a time, beating well after each addition.

Fold in the fruit and flour mixtures alternately. Mix thoroughly. Spoon into a deep 20cm (8in) round cake tin, lined with two layers each of aluminium foil and grease-proof paper. Bake in a moderate oven for 30 minutes. Reduce heat to moderately slow and cook 2½ - 3 hours. Test with a fine skewer before removing from oven.

MOCHA ICE-CREAM

Serves 4

INGREDIENTS

1 x 500ml carton vanilla custard
1 x 300ml container thickened cream
1 teaspoon instant coffee
1 teaspoon gelatine, softened in a little cold water
1 cup grated chocolate
Coffee or chocolate beans
Chocolate liqueur

METHOD

Mix custard and cream together. Place instant coffee and softened gelatine in a small saucepan and stir over a low heat until dissolved. Cool, then stir into cream with grated chocolate.

Freeze quickly. Spoon into sweet dishes, top with beans and pour over liqueur to taste.

CHOCOLATE ICE-CREAM CAKE

Serves 4

INGREDIENTS

4 slices sponge or buttercake
4 scoops vanilla ice-cream

Chocolate fudge sauce:
1 x 100g block dark chocolate
¾ cup cream or evaporated milk
1 egg
½ cup lightly filled brown sugar
1 teaspoon vanilla essence

METHOD

Place cake slices on serving plate and top with generous scoops of ice-cream.

Spoon over chocolate sauce and serve. For a variation, use the chocolate sauce while hot, otherwise chill first, then spoon over ice-cream.

Chocolate Fudge Sauce: Melt chocolate gently in a double saucepan. Beat cream, egg and sugar together and gradually stir into melted chocolate.

Cook over simmering water for 20 minutes, stirring all the time until thickened. Stir in vaniilla essence. Cool. Keeps well in refrigerator for several days. If mixture thickens too much during storage, thin down before using with a little cream or hot water.

NUTTY ANZAC BISCUITS

Makes 30-40

INGREDIENTS

1 cup plain flour
1 cup rolled oats
¾ cup sugar
¼ cup desiccated coconut
½ cup chopped peanuts
2 tablespoons golden syrup
125g (4oz) butter
1 teaspoon bicarbonate of soda
3 tablespoons boiling water

METHOD

Mix the flour, oats, sugar, coconut and peanuts together. Melt the syrup and butter over a gentle heat. Dissolve the bicarbonate of soda in the boiling water, stir in the syrup mixture, and pour over the dry ingredients, stirring until well mixed.

Put heaped teaspoons of the mixture, about 5 cm (2 in) apart to allow for spreading, on greased oven trays. Bake in a moderately slow oven for about 20 minutes. Remove from oven and leave on the trays a few minutes, then lift off with a spatula.

Following pages: Anzac Biscuits (Nutty Anzac Biscuits), recipe this page , and Soldier's Christmas Cake, recipe page 216 were baked by loving wives and mothers to send in food parcels to Australian soldiers fighting overseas in the Great War of 1914-1918.

Light Fruit Cake
Chocolate Candy
Raisin Rolls
Fruit and Oatmeal Cookies
Crystallised Pineapple
Something you have cooked and packed will taste much better to your serviceman
Soldier's Xmas Cake
Lemon Crunches

SORBETS WITH MELON SAUCE

Serves 4-5

KIWI SORBET

INGREDIENTS

6 ripe kiwi fruit
2 tablespoons lemon juice
2 tablespoons icing sugar, sifted

METHOD

Peel kiwi fruit and whizz in a blender until smooth. Stir in lemon juice and icing sugar.

Pour into a freezer-proof bowl and place in freezer. Beat every 15-20 minutes until frozen.

It should be smooth and fluffy.

RASPBERRY SORBET

INGREDIENTS

375g (12oz) fresh or frozen raspberries
¼ cup icing sugar, sifted

METHOD

Pulverise berries in a blender and strain through a fine strainer to remove all seeds.

Stir in icing sugar.

Pour into a freezer-proof bowl and place in freezer. Beat every 15-20 minutes until frozen.

PINEAPPLE SORBET

INGREDIENTS

1 x 450g can crushed pineapple, drained
1 tablespoon lemon juice
1 egg white

METHOD

Place pineapple in a food processor or blender and whizz until smooth. Stir in lemon juice and unbeaten egg white.

Pour into a freezer-proof bowl and place in freezer. Beat every 15-20 minutes until frozen.

MELON SAUCE

INGREDIENTS

4 cups watermelon cubes

METHOD

Take care to remove all seeds from melon. Pulverise in a blender until smooth.

Pour onto individual plates and top with a spoonful of each of the sorbets.

May be served with melon wedges, sliced kiwi fruit, grapes or strawberries dipped in chocolate, tiny cakes or wafer biscuits

Opposite page: Sorbets with Melon Sauce, recipes above.

CREAM PUFFS ROYALE

Makes 20-24

INGREDIENTS

1 cup water
125g (4oz) butter
1 teaspoon sugar
Pinch salt
1 cup plain flour
4 eggs
Whipped, sweetened cream
Icing sugar

METHOD

Place water, butter, sugar and salt in a saucepan and heat until butter melts and liquid is boiling.

Add sifted flour all at once to boiling liquid and stir vigorously with a wooden spoon until mixture comes away from the sides of the saucepan.

Remove from heat and allow to cool for a few minutes. Beat in eggs one at a time until smooth and shiny.

Spoon or pipe mounds onto baking sheets lined with baking paper and cook in a hot oven 20 minutes. Reduce heat to moderately-hot and bake another 10-15 minutes until puffs are golden brown and crisp to touch. Make a small slit in the sides of each puff to allow the steam to escape and return to a warm oven to dry the centres. Cool on wire racks.

Cut tops off puffs and pipe or spoon in the sweetened whipped cream. Replace tops and sieve icing sugar over just before serving.

DUTCH HONEY CAKE

INGREDIENTS

2 cups plain flour
½ teaspoon bicarbonate of soda
1 teaspoon cinnamon
1 teaspoon ground cardamom
1 teaspoon ground ginger
½ teaspoon ground cloves
3 eggs
½ cup vegetable oil
¾ cup honey
¾ cup lightly filled dark brown sugar

Lemond icing: (recipe follows)
Preserved ginger, sliced

METHOD

Sift dry ingredients into large bowl of electric mixer. Add all remaining ingredients and beat 5 minutes.

Pour into a greased 20 cm (8 in) ring cake tin. Bake in a moderate oven until cooked, about 50 minutes. Cool and ice with thin lemon icing and decorate with sliced preserved ginger.

Lemon Icing: Place 1 cup sifted icing sugar into a small saucepan, add 1 teaspoon copha and enough lemon juice to mix to a pouring consistency. Stir over a low heat until copha has melted. Pour over cake and spread to edges.

STRAWBERRIES ARABIA

Serves 2

INGREDIENTS

1 punnet strawberries
1 orange
¼ cup orange brandy liqueur

METHOD

Slice strawberries and place in a serving bowl. Peel rind from orange very thinly with a vegetable peeler and cut into thin strips. Add to strawberries together with the strained orange juice.

Pour over the liqueur, cover and chill 2-3 hours. Delicious with pouring cream or ice-cream.

BLACK FOREST CAKE

INGREDIENTS

1 x 100g block cooking chocolate
125g (4oz) butter
2 cups brown sugar
1 teaspoon vanilla essence
3 eggs
2 cups self-raising flour
Pinch salt
½ teaspoon bicarbonate of soda
¾ cup sour cream
½ cup boiling water

Butter Cream filling and frosting:
250g (8oz) butter
4 cups icing sugar, sifted
2 tablespoons sherry or cherry brandy
½ cup chopped glacé cherries
Chopped walnuts
Whole maraschino cherries

METHOD

Melt chocolate over hot water. Beat together butter, sugar and vanilla essence until creamy. Add eggs one at a time and beat well after each addition. Beat in melted chocolate. Mix in sifted dry ingredients alternately with sour cream and boiling water and beat until smooth.

Divide evenly into 3 greased and base paper-lined 20 cm (8 in) sandwich cake tins and bake in a moderate oven approximately 30 minutes until cooked. Invert onto cake coolers and leave 5 minutes before removing cake tins. These cakes are soft and delicate so handle carefully.

Mix the glacé cherries into a quarter of the butter cream and join the 3 layers together.

Cover top and sides with the remainder, reserving some for piping on the top. Spread smoothly and press chopped walnuts around the outside.

Decorate top by piping swirls of the butter cream around edge and adding a few whole maraschino cherries.

Butter cream filling and frosting: Beat butter until soft and pale. Gradually add icing sugar and sherry or liqueur, beating until smooth and creamy.

NOTE: Morello sour cherries may be used in place of glacé cherries if desired.

The following cakes are legacies from Holland and Germany introduced by the proprietors of European cake shops in the 30's and 40's. The Australian honeybee is also a newcomer, its ancestors coming from Britain in 1822 on the sailing ship Isabella. Following pages: Dutch Honey Cake, left, recipe page 222, and Black Forest Cake, right, recipe above.

FRENCH APPLE TART

Serves 6-8

INGREDIENTS

1 x 375 g packet frozen puff pastry, thawed

4 cooking apples, peeled and sliced thinly

½ cup apricot jam

1 tablespoon white wine or water

METHOD

Roll out pastry into a circle and line a shallow 28 cm (11 in) pie plate or pizza tray.

Cover with apple slices, overlapping and placed close together.

Heat jam and wine together and carefully brush over apple slices. Bake in a hot oven 25-30 minutes, brushing now and again with remaining jam. At the end of cooking time, if desired, place under a hot grill to give a glazed look. Serve warm.

FEDERATION CHARLOTTE

Serves 5-6

INGREDIENTS

16-20 sponge fingers, sides and ends trimmed

1 egg white

1 x 600 ml container thickened cream

2 teaspoons icing sugar

1 tablespoon Grand Marnier or other liqueur

5 teaspoons gelatine

¼ cup orange juice

Red jelly

METHOD

Line a 5-cup mould with oiled greaseproof paper, oiled side down, cut to fit. Arrange sponge fingers evenly around side of mould, packed closely together and long enough to reach top of tin evenly. Brush joins with a little white of egg to seal. Line bottom of mould with sponge fingers, cut in triangles to fit. Whip the cream until thick, add icing sugar and liqueur.

Dissolve the gelatine in the orange juice, cool and stir slowly into the cream, stirring all the time. When mixture begins to thicken pour into the mould. Refrigerate until set. Turn out onto a paper doily on a glass or silver dish, preferably stemmed. Decorate with fresh berries, chopped red jelly and a bow-tied ribbon sash.

Opposite page: French Apple Tart, recipe above.
Following pages: Cream Puffs Royale, recipe page 222; Federation Charlotte, recipe above.

As supplied to
Their Late Majesties
QUEEN VICTORIA
& KING EDWARD VII

PUMPKIN SCONE WEDGE

Makes 8 wedges

INGREDIENTS

2 tablespoons butter
2 tablespoons sugar
1 cup mashed, well-drained, cooked pumpkin
1 egg
2 cups self-raising flour
Pinch salt
⅓ cup sultanas
Milk for glazing

METHOD

Beat together butter and sugar until creamy, mix in the pumpkin and egg.

Sift the flour and salt and mix in, together with the sultanas.

Knead lightly on a floured surface. Pat into a 20 cm (8 in) round and place on a lightly greased oven tray. Cut into 8 sections almost to the bottom so that they can be pulled apart when baked. Brush with milk and bake in a hot oven for 20-25 minutes until cooked.

MILK CHOCOLATE MOUSSE

Serves 4

INGREDIENTS

125 g (4 oz) milk chocolate
3 eggs, separated
1 x 300 ml container thickened cream
Toasted almond slivers
Grated chocolate

METHOD

Melt chocolate gently in a double saucepan. Remove from heat and beat in egg yolks one at a time, beating vigorously.

Beat egg whites until stiff and then whip the cream until thick. Fold chocolate into egg whites and then carefully fold in half the whipped cream.

Alternate layers of chocolate mixture and whipped cream into 4 parfait glasss. Finish with cream on top and chill. Just before serving top with toasted slivered almonds and a little grated chocolate.

Earle Backen.
Still Life. 1982. Watercolour. 118 x 77cm. Bathurst Regional Art Gallery

APPLE CHEESCAKE

Serves 6-8

INGREDIENTS

¾ cup plain flour
60g (2oz) butter, softened
2 teaspoons water
Red jam
2 apples, peeled, cored and sliced
¼ cup sultanas
1 cup cottage cheese, sieved
½ cup plain flour
½ cup sugar
3 eggs
Grated rind 1 lemon
1 tablespoon lemon juice
½ cup cream, whipped

METHOD

Mix flour, butter and water together into a dough. Press evenly onto base of a greased 23 cm (9 in) springform tin. Spread with jam. Cover with apple slices and half the sultanas.

Beat together the cottage cheese, flour, sugar, eggs, lemon rind, juice and the remaining sultanas. Fold in whipped cream and pour over the apples.

Bake in a hot oven 25 minutes until set and top is lightly brown. Sift icing sugar over top and serve warm.

Opposite page: Apple Cheesecake, recipe above.

Index

Lloyd Rees.
Sydney Harbour from Lane Cove.
1981. Oil on canvas. 120 x 140cm.
Bathurst Regional Art Gallery

Art captions

Page 17

Elioth Gruner 1882–1939
Spring Frost 1919
Oil on canvas 131 x 178.7cm
Gift of F.G. White 1939
Art Gallery of New South Wales

This small homestead, built on a free land grant of 30 acres given to convict James Ruse in 1789, was one of the first properties established around Sydney and Parramatta.

It was here that vegetables and fruit were cultivated for the colony, and strawberries were grown from offshoots of a single root that Governor Phillip had brought with him. In 1794 the first plough was introduced, and agriculture began.

Then citrus fruits and many varieties of apples and pears from Tasmania and Victoria became available, enabling industrious housewives to make jams and preserves. Our delicious Apple-Marmalade pie, page 89, could well have been a typical dish of the time.

Page 27

Rupert Bunny 1864–1947
Worked in Europe 1884-1933.
Shrimp Fishers at Saint-Georges (Pêcheurs de crevettes à Saint-Georges) c.1910
Oil on canvas 120.7 x 161.9cm
Felton Bequest 1946
National Gallery of Victoria, Melbourne

Rambles by the sea were favourite family outings in the early days of Australia, just as they still are today. This group of amateur fishers, absorbed by the task of trying to catch some shrimps or small prawns, would probably have been disappointed, but they present a charming picture just the same. Prawns have always been regarded as a delicacy in Australia, despite their abundance. Fresh prawns were sold in the streets of Sydney in the 1850s for sixpence a pint. Since then, they have gradually become an expensive luxury, only to be eaten on special occasions. Prawn cocktails have been popular first courses for decades, and buckets of prawns are often served at parties and barbecues, or on the peculiarly Australian "prawn night" celebrations in pubs.

Page 39

Graham Lupp 1983

Chickens
Watercolour 29 x 50 cm
Private Collection

The poor inhabitants of this tumbledown little house would probably have lived on mutton, bread and tea, the staple diet of early Australian settlers. During the Depression, baked or stewed rabbit was a cheap sustaining meal. A dish of chicken varied the monotony, but only on special occasions such as Sundays, Easter and Christmas. Elaborately sauced frenchified poultry dishes were fashionable restaurant and banquet fare for moneyed people. Among the working classes, English style roast chicken with stuffing, bread sauce and roast vegetables became a popular Sunday midday dinner which gradually declined as supermarket battery chickens became cheap and plentiful.

Page 51

Sali Herman b. 1898

Near the Docks 1949
Oil on canvas 50.7 x 96.8cm
purchased 1949
Art Gallery of New South Wales

Dishes such as Irish stew and cooked pigís trotters would probably have been popular among the original residents of these simple workmenís cottages and terrace houses in old Sydney Town. Streets such as this one proliferated as immigrants poured into Australia in the 19th century looking for work and possible wealth. The well-to-do lived in larger houses with gardens and enjoyed a basically British diet from the better cuts of meat. Our recipe for Gentlemanís Breakfast on page 80 could have been prepared in the kitchens of a merchant or businessmanís house or club, maybe a lodging house or hotel, as a variation on the adopted porridge, lamb chop, bacon and eggs, toast and marmalade breakfast fare of England.

Page 71

Page 123

Hugh Ramsay 1877-1906
The Sisters, 1904
Oil on canvas on hardboard 125.7 x 144.8cm
purchased 1921
Art Gallery of New South Wales

The artistis sisters sitting so petulantly in their satin and tulle gowns in Hugh Ramsayis painting above are obviously well-to-do turn-of-the-century Australians. Have they just returned from a ball? Are they going to one of the elaborate banquets so popular at the time? Perhaps they are waiting for their carriage to take them to the opera or the theatre. In any case they would undoubtedly indulge in many sumptuous meals of rich party food ending with the sweet French or English puddings which were so popular at the time.

John Skinner Prout 1806-1876
(Bush landscape with waterfall and an aborigine stalking native animals, New South Wales, 1860's)
Oil on canvas 70.5 x 91.4cm
Purchased under the terms of the Florence Turner Blake bequest 1976
Art Gallery of New South Wales

Page 87

William Ford c.1820–c.1886

Born Great Britain (c.1820), arrived in Australia (c.1870), died (c.1886)
At the Hanging Rock 1875
Oil on canvas 79.2 x 117.5cm
purchased 1950
National Gallery of Victoria, Melbourne

Australians have always loved picnics. Eating outdoors was borne of necessity in the earliest days of the colony when shelter was scarce and dining rooms nonexistent. But the taste for eating outside lingered, developed and then flourished long after there was housing for all, however grand or humble.

Would the picnickers here have ever guessed that their day's outing would be celebrated a hundred years later as the title of a famous Australian film adapted from the novel "Picnic at Hanging Rock" ? They would have travelled to the high country outside Melbourne, Victoria, by coach, wagonette or train and then reached the strange bushland with its tall trees on Foot. The food brought with them was most likely modelled on the picnic provisions popularised in the 1860s by Mrs Beaton and her book. Pies, fruit cakes and a huge selection of cold foods in staggering proportions were deemed correct fare for such an occasion whether it be in England, India or any of the British colonies.

Page 135

David Strachan 1919–1970
Fish, 1953
Oil on wood 37.8 x 40.7cm
purchased 1954
Art Gallery of New South Wales

Page 151

Ena Joyce
After Lunch 1982
Gouache 37.5 x 55cm
Bathurst Regional Art Gallery

Page 173

Ethel Spowers
Australia 1890–1947
Bank Holiday 1935
Colour linocut 24.6 x 25.0cm
Felton Bequest 1937
National Gallery of Victoria, Melbourne

The average Australian enjoys many long weekends througshout the year. National, memorial, commercial and religious days are often tacked on to weekends to shorten numerous working weeks. Any opportunity to escape from the routine of work to the beach or the bush is welcomed, often with blissful disregard for the original reason for the holiday.

The family-style picnic portrayed in this linocut shows a group of people temporarily free from the cares of life as they were at the time; the still difficult period of economic recovery after the Depression. They are obviously relaxed and happy and preparing to enjoy an alfresco meal which seems to consist of billy tea, sandwiches, cakes, beer and a pineapple.

Page 193

Elayne Russell
Figs and Capsicums 1983
Pastel on paper 65.5 x 99.5cm
Bathurst Regional Art Gallery

Page 201

Jean Bellette

Still Life with Wooden Bowl, [date unknown]
Oil on hardboard 54.6 x 81.3cm
purchased 1954
Art Gallery of New South Wales
© AGNSW

Page 212

Grace Cossington-Smith 1892-1984

The Lacquer Room, 1935-1936
Oil on paperboard on plywood 74 x 90.8cm
purchased 1967
Art Gallery of New South Wales
© AGNSW

In the 1930s eating in restaurants was usually out of the question. For the hard-up, even a simple meal in a cheap restaurant was an extravagance; probably steak and eggs or a Chinese meal were the ultimate weekend treat. Lunchtime sandwiches were usually replaced by a light lunchtime snack in a tearoom or coffee shop where they mingled with commercial travellers or tired housewives on shopping trips to the city.

The bare tables and sparse Art Deco trim of the cafe in this painting accurately illustrate the mood of the time. This feeling is further emphasised by the impersonal attitudes of the waitresses and the lonely almost desperate expressions on the faces of the customers.

Bibliography

Old Days: Old Ways by Mary Gilmore
Sirius Books,
Angus & Robertson Ltd.
First published in June, 1934
First published by Sirius in 1963

Our Home in Australia
A Description of Cottage
Life in 1860 by Joseph Elliott
The Flannel Flower Press,
Sydney, 1984

One Continuous Picnic
A History of Eating in Australia
by Michael Symons
Penguin Books, 1984

Colonial Food & Drink 1788–1901
Published by the Historic Houses
Trust of New South Wales in
conjunction with an exhibition
at Elizabeth Bay House,
December 1985 – May 1986

Australia As Once We Were by John Ritchie
William Heinemann Australia
Pty. Ltd. 1975

Advice to a Young Lady in the Colonies being a letter sent from Mrs. E of England to Maria Macarthur in the Colony of New South Wales in 1812
Greenhouse Publications
Pty. Ltd., 1979

The Shearers by Patsy Adam-Smith
Nelson, 1982

Beeton's Book of Household Management
Originally published in London
by S.O. Beeton, 1861
Reproduced by Jonathan Cape
Limited, London, 1968

MEASUREMENTS

Recipe measurements in this book are given in metric units with imperial units in brackets. Use either metric or imperial measurements, but never mix them. Australian standard metric measuring spoons and cups are used in the recipes in this book. Eggs are 55 g size.
1 Australian metric cup is 250 ml.
1 Australian metric tablespoon is 20 ml.
1 Australian metric teaspoon is 5 ml.

TEMPERATURES

	°C	°F	Gas Mark
Very slow	120	250	1
Slow	150	300	2
Mod slow	160	325	3
Moderate	180	350	4
Mod hot	190(g) – 210(e)	375 – 425	5
Hot	200(g) – 240(e)	400 – 475	6
Very hot	230(g) – 260(e)	450 – 525	8

(g) = gas (e) = electric